Karl Michael Popp (ed.):

Automating the Deal:
How Disruptive Tools Are Transforming M&A Forever

Impressum

Bibliografische Information der Deutschen Nationalbibliothek
Die Deutsche Nationalbibliothek verzeichnet diese Publikation in der
Deutschen Nationalbibliografie; detaillierte bibliografische Daten sind
im Internet über http://dnb.d-nb.de abrufbar.

Verlag: BoD · Books on Demand GmbH, In de Tarpen 42,
22848 Norderstedt, bod@bod.de
Druck: Libri Plureos GmbH, Friedensallee 273, 22763 Hamburg
ISBN-13: 978-3-7693-7877-1

Disclaimer

Copyright © 2025 Dr. Karl Popp

Karl Michael Popp (ed.): Automating the Deal Vol. 1

OVERVIEW OF CONTENT

Contents

1. Introduction

Dr. Karl Michael Popp

In the age of hyper-automation and artificial intelligence, it is paramount to leverage extreme levels of automation wherever possible. This book is intended to show which unique automation is possible today using state-of-the-art tools.

1.1 Problem statement

M&A strategy professionals don´t have an overview over different tools that can be used for automation of the M&A process. They don´t have the time to get a proper and trusted evaluation of which parts of the M&A processes can already be automated today. Think about automatic supply chain and customer chain analysis, automatic revenue predictions, automatic prediction of patent exploitation potential and more.

This book addresses innovative automation scenarios for the M&A process by showing which activities can be automated by different tools in a disruptive manner. They allow practitioners to select the right tools.

Based on evaluations of many tools over a four-year period, the best and most disruptive tools were chosen to be presented in this book. It is based on four tools that are the base offering of corpvision.ai. Two of the tools, ABRAMS world trade wiki and PATEV are covered in this book.

1.2 Target Audience of the Book

Target Audience of the book are M&A leads and professionals, managers and employees of strategy departments, corporate development departments and M&A departments, consultants and advisors in the M&A space, and persons responsible for post-merger integration as well as students and teachers in the field of M&A.

This book can be used as follows:

Identify the tasks to be digitized: This book describes almost all tasks of the M&A strategy definition phase. The tasks relevant for a company can be selected and then automated in a targeted manner.

Overview of automation scenarios for the M&A process: The automatability described for the tasks provides an overview of which tasks in the M&A process can already be automated today.

Foundation to select the right tools: the scenarios allow practitioners to select tools based on the information that is relevant to them: automating the process in a way that creates value.

1.3 Content of the book

Chapter two introduces M&A processes and their automation. Chapters three to five introduce the M&A strategy phase of the M&A process and contain automation scenarios leveraging tools.

Chapters six to eight show the details and automation scenarios for the due diligence phase. Chapters nine to 11 deal with the merger integration phase and its automation. Chapter 12 introduces the companies behind the scenarios in this book. Chapter 13 provides an outlook by providing a vision of M&A automation in the near future.

1.4 Acknowledgement

This book would not have been possible without the support of several helpers, supporters and experts. A big thank you goes to the authors of the different chapters of this book.

I am always receptive and grateful for feedback, please send it by email to karl_popp@hotmail.com.

If you like, contact me on Linkedin.

And, if you consider selling your profitable software company, get in touch with me.

https://www.linkedin.com/in/drkarlmichaelpopp/

2. Merger Automation

Dr. Karl Michael Popp

This section dives into topics around automatability and automation of tasks in the M&A process. We will look at some concepts regarding automation, but also at technologies available these days to automate tasks in the M&A process. If you are interested in more details, please have a look at my other books on this subject [Popp,20], [Popp,23].

2.1 Automation goals and requirements for the M&A process

Goal of the automation of the M&A process

The goal of automation of the M&A process is the continuous data and application-integrated (partial) automation of all tasks and phases of the process. Today, the tool landscape for M&A is highly fragmented. Due to the many automation islands, caused by isolated use of single tools, an open architecture is required by which the various tools can be integrated based on standardized interfaces. Now, let us look at automation requirements and business requirements.

Automation requirements

We have the following automation requirements.

Consistent automation of processes

Companies often have processes that are not fully (partially) automated. But what does continuous automation mean? This can be defined by considering the integration of tasks by machine, software, and personnel.

If the same automated task owners, such as application systems, are assigned to several consecutive tasks, this sequence of tasks is machine integrated. If the same personnel task objects are assigned to several consecutive tasks, the tasks are called personnel integrated tasks.

Maximum use of available technologies

Where the use of technology makes sense, such technology should be used to drive up the level of automation as much as possible.

Business requirements

We have five business requirements.

Process standardization and optimization

Automation can raise the efficiency of a business process. To maximize the effect, M&A processes should be standardized. Higher degrees of optimization can support business experts in focusing on the decision-making process, not on the data collection or data display. Later in the book, we will show that support for decisions can also be largely automated.

Bias and noise control and elimination

Cognitive bias and bias in application system adversely impact the quality of decision making. Both types of bias should be avoided with the help of tools.

Getting around missing data

Some machine learning algorithms can cope perfectly with missing data. They can estimate or extrapolate missing data to complete information about a company or its attributes.

Organizational optimization

We must make the best use of the experts in the workforce. New automation options and scenarios change the division of work between experts and advanced tools.

Create value for the M&A professional

That is maybe the most important requirement, since value creation motivates professionals to use the tools. Tools must make things easier, faster, more accurate; otherwise, they are of no use. With new technologies, the tools can also offer new, disruptive ways to automate M&A tasks, which we will show in this book in later chapters.

2.2 Automation and Automatability of Tasks

Decisions on the digitization of companies depend on the available implementation options. The goal is the extensive and meaningful automation of operational tasks. This section is taken from [Popp,20].

Automation of tasks

To fully automate a business process, both the tasks and the coupling of tasks within the process must be fully automated. In addition to full automation, there are other degrees of automation. The degrees of automation of tasks can be distinguished by the assignment of combinations of task owner types to tasks in Figure 1 [cf. FeSi, 97].

The available task owner types are personnel task owners (humans) and mechanical task owners (computers, automats, robots, software). If only personnel task owners are assigned to a task, it

If both personnel and tools, are jointly assigned to a task, the task is called semi-automated. A task is called fully automated (automated) if it is assigned exclusively to tools (automated task owners).

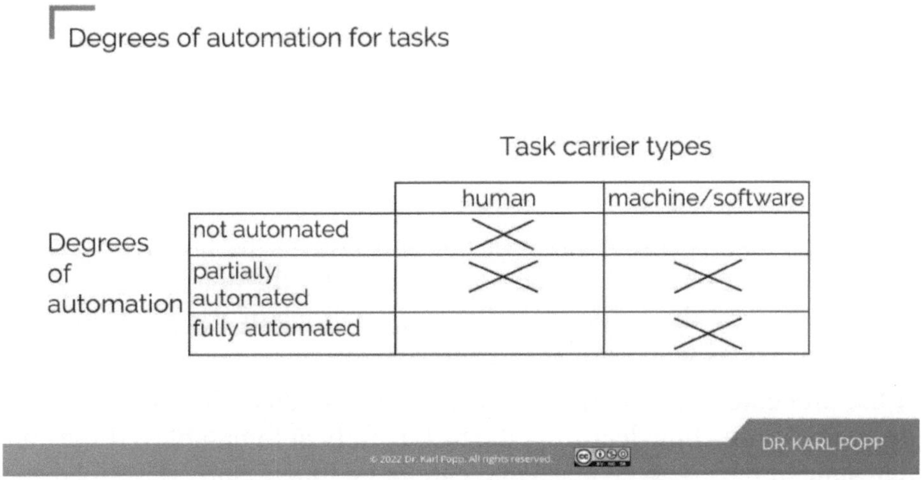

Degrees of automation for tasks

Degrees of automation		human	machine/software
	not automated	✕	
	partially automated	✕	✕
	fully automated		✕

Task carrier types

Figure 1: Degrees of automation of tasks, source: [FeSi,97]

Automated and semi-automated tasks and the associated application systems are relevant for digitization. In this book they are summarized under the term (partially) automated tasks.

Before a task can be automated, the automatability of the tasks must be clarified. Only a task that is automatable can be automated.

Automatability of tasks

A procedure describes the execution of a task from an internal perspective. It consists of a set of actions that are linked together and controlled by an action control.

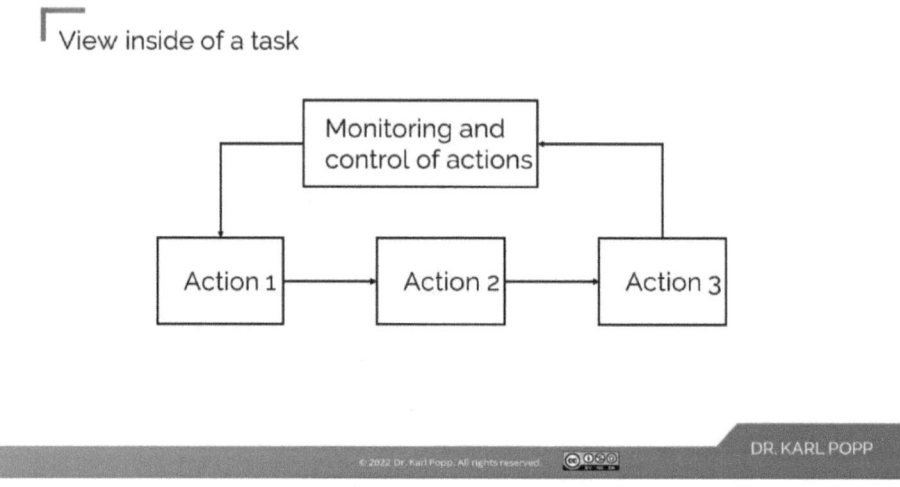

Figure 2: Actions and action control, source: FeSi93

Whether a task is automatable or not depends on the properties of the procedure for executing a task. More precisely: the automatability can be described by the automatability of all actions of the procedure for solving a task as well as of the action control.

If the procedure for solving a task can be described algorithmically or by means of machine learning, the task is fully automatable. At the current state of the art, even tasks that cannot be functionally described can be automated (so-called decision tasks) using data science or machine learning approaches.

Many decision tasks that in the past could only be carried out by personnel, can now be fully automated. One example is an automated analysis of contract texts for specific features based on algorithms for natural language analysis. Today, action control can also be at least partially automated. Workflow systems, project control software or even data rooms with action control are available for action control.

Example

Let us have a look at one of our tasks, Finding potential targets.

The task Finding potential targets consists of four actions. Let us have a look at how automated this task could be executed. Based on limited market research, say, 16 Tools are available for this task. Each of the tools automates one or more of the actions of this task.

Here's the overview of actions and corresponding automation if tools are used. Here, a total of 17 tools were analyzed:

❏ Define selection criteria and market is automated by 7 tool(s).

❏ Scan sources for potential targets is automated by 3 tool(s).

❏ Review companies to join the longlist is automated by 5 tool(s).

❏ Define the longlist of targets is automated by 8 tool(s).

This task is clearly partially automatable. Using one of the tools allows the task to be partially automated or, if the tool automates all actions, fully automated.

Finding potential targets

This task is partially automatable.

Goals

Longlist of targets created

Objectives

Information asymmetry minimized, Buyer-target complementarity maximized

Task Description

With the result from the previous task, you have defined a space to search in and you have put requirements in place that the potential target should fulfill. First, finding targets requires a selection of the right sources to search for targets. You can look for acquisition targets in the company ecosystem, e.g. partners, suppliers, customers, competitors and in adjacent or remote markets. You can use service providers and company search databases to find appropriate targets. The search process might be iterative, so you might start with searching targets that fulfill only a few attributes, like e.g. strategy fit, size/revenue, target market fit. If you end up with a large amount of companies, you start the second iteration trying to fulfill additional attributes like business model fit, business scalability, technology fit or other attributes. Objectives of the task steer your work. You try to minimize information asymmetry by using several sources. In addition, you try to maximize the complementarity between buyer and target.

Due to incomplete information, it cannot be guaranteed that all existing, suitable targets are known to the purchasing company. For this reason, a basic set is created with the help of various sources of information, such as databases, industry experts and information on start-ups. When targets have been found, this is followed by detailed walkthrough of target candidates and a decision according to various criteria such as target competencies, region/location, sales, company size and technology attractiveness, which candidates make it onto the longlist of potential targets. From this set, companies are selected for the long list.

Subtasks of the Task

Task consists of the actions

Define selection criteria and market, not automatable. Scan sources for potential targets, automatable. Review companies to join the longlist, partially automatable. Define the longlist of targets, partially automatable

Data objects

Target, Buyer, Target countries, Assignment of target markets to industry, Buyer Industry, Market of the target, Market of the buyer, Target company, Target locations, Longlist of targets, Ecosystem, Ecosystem of the buyer, Product of the target, Product of the buyer, Sales of the target, Target employees, Target business model, Buyer business model, Target business, Buyer business, Analyst company, Buy Side Advisor, Sell-side advisor, Market, Market Drivers, Customer of the buyer, Customer of the target, Supplier of the buyer, Supplier of the target, Partner of the buyer, Partner of the target, Buyer-partner value proposition, Competitor of the buyer, Target Competitor, Buyer-target complementarity, Cost Complementarity, Product complementarity, Market Complementarity, Supply chain complementarity, Complementarity of the strategy, Complementarity of the GTM model, Brand complementarity, Target ecosystem strategy complementarity, Business model complementarity, Patent of the target, Patent, Patent of the buyer, Patent portfolio complementarity, Complementarity of countries, Financial complementarity, Complementarity of resource models, Service of the buyer, Service of the target, Services complementarity

Task supported by the tools

World Trade Wiki, Patev, Alphasense, Arx Platform, Delphai, Dealcircle, Deloitte Target Screening app, Digimind, Equintel, EY Embryonic, ITONICS Scout, MA Discover, Nexis, Orbis Database, Palturai, Proseeder, TargetIQ, Valu8, vencortex M&A

Display AOS   Ok

Figure 3: A Tasks and its actions in the M&A reference model

2.3   Technologies for the M&A process

In this section, we list technologies and give examples of how they can be used during M&A processes. These technologies include compliance and audit technology, collaboration technology, data science technology, deployment options, document processing technology, integration technology, machine learning technology, natural language processing technology, process automation technology, security technology, education and training content, and agent technology.

Compliance and audit technology

Audit trail

A data store with audit trail writes and keeps logs of any access to certain data and any activity of users with the data residing in the data store. An audit trail contains information about who accessed which information at which point in time.

One way to utilize an audit trail during a merger or acquisition is to use it to track changes to access controls. When bringing two companies together, there may be a need to update or modify access privileges for various systems or platforms. This can be done through IT departments, and the changes should always be thoroughly recorded in an audit trail. This will help ensure that sensitive data remains secure and that changes to access don't go unnoticed.

In addition to tracking access control changes, audit trails can also be used to monitor user activity. This can be especially useful during a merger or acquisition when there may be a higher risk of unauthorized access or data breaches. By tracking user activity, businesses can quickly identify potential threats and take swift action to mitigate them.

Finally, audit trails can be used to ensure compliance with regulations and legal requirements. Many industries have specific regulations that businesses must abide by, and this is especially true during mergers and acquisitions when there may be new regulatory requirements introduced. Consequently, audit trails that track activities can help ensure that businesses remain in compliance with these regulations and avoid any potential fines or legal action.

Summing up, an audit trail can be a tremendously valuable tool during mergers and acquisitions. By tracking changes to access controls, monitoring user activity, and ensuring compliance with regulations, audit trails can provide businesses with a greater level of security and confidence during times of change. If you're planning a merger or acquisition, be sure to consider the benefits of an audit trail and take steps to implement one.

Collaboration technology

Telephony

Telephony refers to the technology and infrastructure used for voice communication over a distance. This includes traditional telephone systems, as well as more recent technologies such as Voice over Internet Protocol (VoIP) and cellular networks. Telephony systems use a variety of technologies to transmit and receive voice signals, such as circuit-switched telephone networks, packet-switched networks, and wireless networks. Telephony also includes the use of software and hardware to manage and route calls, as well as features such as voicemail, call forwarding, and conference calls. Telephony is widely used for both personal and business communication and has evolved over time to include new technologies like videoconferencing, messaging, and internet-based services.

Telephony can help you streamline communication and collaboration during the merger or acquisition process. First, telephony allows for seamless communication between teams regardless of location. With features like video conferencing and VoIP, team members can communicate in real-time, regardless of where they are in the world. This makes it easier for teams to collaborate, review documents together, and ask questions that may arise in the process. Telephony also allows for quick and efficient communication with stakeholders. During a merger or acquisition, stakeholders need to be informed of any changes or updates quickly. Using telephony ensures that everyone has access to the information they need, reducing delays and miscommunication. Furthermore, telephony can facilitate the integration process post-merger or acquisition. By using tools like a company-wide phone system, teams can communicate efficiently and seamlessly with one another, creating a smooth transition for all involved. Overall, the use of telephony technology during mergers and acquisitions can save time, reduce cost, and improve overall communication.

Whiteboarding

Whiteboarding refers to the process of creating visual diagrams, illustrations, or sketches on a whiteboard, which is typically a large, erasable surface that can be written on with dry-erase markers. Whiteboarding can be used for a variety of purposes, such as brainstorming, problem-solving, and team collaboration. It allows users to visually organize and present information, and to easily make changes and revisions. Whiteboarding can be done in person, using a physical whiteboard, or remotely, using digital whiteboarding software, which allows users to collaborate and share their work in real-time, regardless of their physical location. It is a popular tool in many fields such as education, business, and design, as it allows us to easily explain complex ideas, and be more interactive. Here, we refer to digital whiteboarding only.

Using whiteboards allows teams to collaborate and brainstorm in real-time, which can help improve communication, identify potential issues, and develop solutions. In the context of mergers and acquisitions, whiteboarding can be incredibly valuable. Here are some ways it can help:

Identify goals and priorities: Before a merger or acquisition takes place, it's important to identify the goals and priorities of both organizations. Whiteboarding can help teams visualize these goals and prioritize them so that everyone is on the same page.

Explore different scenarios: Whiteboarding allows teams to brainstorm different scenarios and potential outcomes. This can help in negotiations and decision-making as the team can evaluate the pros and cons of each scenario.

Map out key details: There are often many details to consider when it comes to mergers and acquisitions, such as legal requirements, financial due diligence, and cultural integration. Whiteboarding can help teams map out these key details in a clear and organized way.

Facilitate communication: Whiteboarding encourages open communication and collaboration among team members. This can be especially helpful in the context of mergers and acquisitions where different teams may be working together for the first time. In summary, whiteboarding can be a powerful tool in the context of mergers and acquisitions. By visualizing complex ideas, exploring different scenarios, mapping out key details, and facilitating communication, teams can work together more effectively to unlock the growth potential of the transaction.

Chat

Chat functionality is the ability of a computer program or a device to exchange messages with a human user or another computer program in a conversational style. Chat functionality is often used in messaging apps, online customer service systems, and social media platforms to allow users to communicate with each other in real-time. In a chat system, users can send and receive text messages, files, and other media as part of a conversation. Chat functionality can also include features such as emoticons, GIFs, and other interactive elements to make the conversation more engaging.

Using chat functionality is a quick and efficient way to communicate and collaborate in real-time. Chat tools such as Microsoft Teams, Slack, and WhatsApp can greatly aid in collaboration amongst teams from different companies.

During mergers and acquisitions, chat can be used to create channels where teams can share information in real-time. This way, everyone can be kept up to date on the progress of the integration. Additionally, chat rooms can be created for specific project teams where they can share goals, timelines, and deliverables. Another advantage of using chat is that it creates a level playing field for everyone. In most mergers and acquisitions, one company is usually stronger, and communication can be skewed in their favor. With chat, however, all team members can share their opinions and thoughts without feeling intimidated, leading to more effective communication. Finally, chat tools are just as effective for team-building activities. During the merger or acquisition process, it's critical to build a culture where all employees feel valued and appreciated. Creating chat rooms for socializing and bonding activities can foster positive relationships amongst the teams from different companies. In conclusion, communication is vital during mergers and acquisitions. Chat tools provide a quick and efficient way to communicate and collaborate in real-time. Using chat to create channels, chat rooms, and for team building can foster effective communication leading to successful integrations.

Collaboration rooms

Collaboration rooms are virtual spaces where people can come together to work on a project or task. These spaces may be equipped with technology such as videoconferencing and screen sharing to help people communicate and work together effectively. They are often used by organizations to improve productivity, foster creativity, and encourage collaboration among employees, partners, and customers.

Collaboration rooms are designed to facilitate meetings, keep everyone in sync, and help disparate teams merge into one cohesive unit. are especially useful when teams are located in different parts of the globe and can help reduce the time and cost associated with travel. So, how can you put collaboration rooms to good use during mergers and acquisitions?

Bring everyone together for regular meetings - This ensures that everyone is on the same page and that progress is being made.

Use collaboration rooms to foster open and honest communication - Encourage employees to speak up and share their ideas, concerns and feedback.

Ensure that all teams have access to the collaboration tools - This will help ensure a smooth and seamless transition between different teams. In conclusion, collaboration rooms are an essential tool for mergers and acquisitions. They can help bring disparate teams together, foster open communication, and ensure that the transition is as smooth as possible.

Virtual meetings

Virtual meetings are meetings which are conducted between people in different locations using a tool. The tool connects and allows communication between team members in different locations using videoconferencing, chat and voice calls.

Virtual meetings break down communication barriers by allowing stakeholders to meet over the internet from anywhere in the world. Additionally, virtual meetings help break down communication silos, ensuring that everyone involved in the M&A is on the same page.

Traditional M&A processes come with high travel costs. Virtual meetings eliminate this cost while still delivering the same results as face-to-face meetings. Virtual meetings are cost-effective, especially when participants are located far apart or in different countries.

Virtual meetings provide the flexibility of scheduling meetings at times that are convenient for all participants, regardless of their location. This is particularly helpful when dealing with stakeholders in different time zones. Virtual meetings also require less preparation time, eliminating the need for extensive travel arrangements.

Virtual meetings make it easier and faster to gather and analyze data. This leads to informed decision-making and better outcomes.

Data science technology

Automatic identification of missing data

One important issue in M&A is missing data, e.g., if there are no contracts for a customer in a data room. If a tool allows us to find missing data without human intervention, we call this automatic alerting of missing data.

A simple example is a due diligence folder structure that contains folders for documents provided by the target company. If the tool used to store the data automatically alerts that empty folders exist, we can call this automatic alerting of missing data.

Automated identification of missing data refers to the process of using computer algorithms to identify and locate missing data in a dataset. This can be a useful tool for organizations that have large amounts of data and need to ensure that their datasets are complete and accurate. There are a variety of approaches that can be used for automated finding of missing data, including machine learning algorithms and statistical methods. Some common applications for automated finding of missing data include imputing missing values, detecting errors or inconsistencies in data, and identifying trends or patterns in data.

Document classification

Automatic classification of documents refers to the process of using algorithms and machine learning techniques to automatically categorize text documents into predefined categories or classes. This is typically done by training a machine learning model on a dataset of labeled documents, where each document is associated with one or more classes. Once the model is trained, it can be used to classify new, unseen documents based on their content. This can be done by extracting features from the document, such as words, phrases, or other linguistic features, and then using these features as input to the model. The output of the model is a prediction of the class or classes that best match the document. Automatic document classification can be used for a variety of tasks, such as text categorization, sentiment analysis, or spam detection, and is widely used in fields such as natural language processing, information retrieval and machine learning to process huge amounts of data.

Proper document classification is essential during M&A for three reasons. First, it enables efficient due diligence. Due diligence is an essential phase of the M&A process, where the acquirer examines the company being acquired to identify any risks, legal or financial issues, or potential opportunities. Document classification can help consolidate and organize the massive amounts of data that must be reviewed as part of this process. This helps ensure that all relevant information is available for review, expediting the due diligence process.

Second, document classification helps ensure compliance with regulatory requirements. Many sectors, such as healthcare or finance, have specific rules regarding data handling and protection. Ensuring that all documents are properly classified according to these guidelines can prevent any regulatory mishaps that could slow down or even derail the M&A process.

Third, proper document classification allows for optimal integration of systems and processes. In M&A, the two companies must integrate their technologies and processes to enable their efficient operation as an integrated entity. If the documents are not properly classified, the integration process could take much longer and require additional resources.

In conclusion, document classification is essential in M&A as it allows for efficient due diligence, ensures compliance with regulatory requirements, and enables optimal integration of systems and processes.

Simple Analytics

Simple analytics refers to the process of collecting, analyzing, and interpreting data to gain insights and make better decisions. Analytics can be applied to a wide range of data, including structured data from databases, as well as unstructured data from sources such as social media, text documents, and sensor data. One example is a pie chart showing the distribution of revenue among products and services.

Advanced analytics

Advanced analytics is the use of sophisticated data analysis techniques and tools to extract insights and knowledge from data. These techniques often go beyond simple statistical analysis and may include machine learning algorithms, data mining, or natural language processing or a combination of them. The goal of advanced analytics is to uncover patterns and relationships in data that can be used to make informed decisions and predictions. Advanced analytics is often used in industries such as finance, healthcare, and marketing to improve decision making and drive business growth. It includes data manipulation, data transformation, knowledge extraction and non-biased decision making.

Fortunately, advanced analytics can provide valuable insights to navigate these challenges and maximize the potential of M&A. The primary use of advanced analytics during M&A is to gain a deeper understanding of the data of the target company. This includes analyzing their performance, operations, customers, and financials. The analysis should be done before the deal is finalized, during the integration process, and even post-integration to measure the effectiveness of the merger.

One of the primary benefits of using advanced analytics in M&A is that it allows for a detailed assessment of the target company's operations.

This analysis can identify any inefficiencies, overlaps, or redundancies that can be streamlined.

Advanced analytics also allow for a granular level of understanding of the target company's customers and preferences, which can be used to cross-sell and upsell services. Another essential use of advanced analytics during M&A is to understand the target company's financial health. This includes analyzing their cash flow, revenue, expenses, and debt. By understanding the financial position of the target company, organizations can make better-informed decisions and avoid any unwelcome surprises post-integration.

Lastly, advanced analytics can help with aligning cultures during the integration process. By analyzing employee data, such as work habits, communication patterns, and values, organizations can create a cohesive culture that incorporates the best of both companies. Ultimately, advanced analytics can provide unique insights that can help organizations maximize the potential of M&A.

Augmented analytics

Augmented analytics is a subtype of data analytics that uses artificial intelligence (AI) and machine learning to automate the process of analyzing and visualizing data plus augmenting these data with additional data and information or suggestions that might make sense in the given user context.

The goal of augmented analytics is to make data analytics more accessible to a wider range of people, so that organizations can make data-driven decisions more quickly and easily. An example is looking at revenue data and revenue growth of a target. Augmented analytics also provide data about target markets' growth as well as the revenue data and growth of competitors.

Augmented analytics refers to the use of machine learning algorithms and artificial intelligence to automate the process of data discovery, analysis, and insights. By utilizing advanced technologies and predictive models, augmented analytics can rapidly process large amounts of data, identify patterns, and provide valuable insights for companies undergoing mergers and acquisitions.

One of the biggest advantages of augmented analytics is that it can help businesses identify synergies between two companies, which is especially helpful during a merger or acquisition. By analyzing and matching data on topics such as customer behavior, sales revenue, and product lines, augmented analytics can pinpoint areas of overlap and opportunities for growth.

Another benefit of augmented analytics is that it can help businesses reduce cost and increase profitability. By analyzing financial data, the technology can identify areas where the business can cut cost or increase revenue, such as minimizing duplicated efforts, identifying supply chain inefficiencies, or adjusting pricing strategies.

Furthermore, augmented analytics can also help businesses avoid potential risks during mergers and acquisitions. By analyzing risk factors such as vendor performance, regulatory compliance, and financial stability, augmented analytics can help companies make more informed decisions and avoid costly mistakes. In conclusion, augmented analytics are becoming an essential tool for companies looking to navigate the complexities of mergers and acquisitions.

Detection of anomalies

Anomaly detection is the automatic process of identifying irregularities, which are unusual patterns in data that do not conform to expected patterns. This is often used to detect fraud, network intrusions, or other unusual events that may require further investigation. Anomaly detection algorithms can be trained using historical data, and then used to identify anomalies in real-time data streams. These algorithms can be used in a variety of fields, including finance, manufacturing, and cybersecurity.

One of the critical areas where detection of anomalies can be helpful is in the due diligence process. Due diligence is a thorough investigation of a company's health, and it is an essential step before closing any M&A transaction. Anomalies in financial statements, such as inconsistent revenue or expense patterns, could indicate accounting irregularities and raise red flags.

Similarly, anomalies in legal documents, including pending lawsuits or regulatory issues, could indicate potential liabilities that need to be addressed. Another way to use detection of anomalies in M&A transactions is to identify potential cultural mismatches. Differences in company culture and values can undermine the success of an M&A. By analyzing data on employee engagement, retention, and turnover rates, you can identify potential culture clashes early and take steps to mitigate them.

Using detection of anomalies can also help you identify potential risks and opportunities for cost savings. Anomaly detection tools can analyze vast amounts of data, including customer behavior, operational data, and supply chain information. By identifying anomalies in these areas, you can gain insights into potential risks and opportunities for cost savings. For example, identifying anomalous supplier prices or payment terms could help you negotiate better deals and reduce costs. In conclusion, the detection of anomalies can be a powerful tool to help manage the complex and risky process of M&A transactions.

By identifying risks and opportunities early on, companies can make more informed decisions, reduce costs, and improve their chances of success.

Detection of patterns

Pattern detection is the process of identifying patterns, or regularities, in data. This can involve identifying patterns in a single dataset or finding relationships between multiple datasets. Pattern detection can be used in a variety of fields, including data mining, machine learning, and statistical analysis. It is a key part of many data-driven processes, as it allows us to discover useful insights and relationships in data that may not be immediately apparent.

Here are some ways in which detection of patterns can be leveraged during M&A:

Identifying Red Flags: One of the primary uses of pattern detection is identifying any red flags that might prevent an M&A from being successful. Potential issues could include operational inefficiencies, compatibility issues with leadership styles, or cultural mismatches.

Identifying these potential problems early in the process allows for solutions to be put in place before they become major issues.

Predicting Future Trends: Patterns in data can help to predict future trends in the industry. By analyzing market trends and identifying patterns of consumer behavior, businesses can position themselves for future success.

Better Resource Allocation: The detection of patterns in M&A can also enable businesses to allocate resources more effectively. By analyzing data, businesses can identify areas of overlap and redundancy, and then optimize resources to reduce costs and improve productivity.

Improved Decision-Making: The ability to identify patterns during M&A can lead to better decision-making. By analyzing patterns and predicting future trends, businesses can make more informed choices about where to invest their time, money, and resources. In conclusion, the detection of patterns is an essential tool for companies looking to successfully navigate the M&A process. It allows for better resource allocation, improved decision-making, and the identification of potential issues before they become major problems.

Deployment options

Supported hyperscalers

This attribute tells which major infrastructure as a service providers (so called hyperscalers) can be used. Examples are Microsoft, Google, Amazon, Alibaba.

Document processing technology

Document versioning

Document versioning refers to the process of keeping track of changes made to a document over time and maintaining a history of all versions of the document. This process allows users to see and compare different versions of the document and revert to a previous version if necessary. Document versioning can be done manually, by manually saving copies of a document with different names or file extensions, or automatically, by using software that tracks changes and saves new versions automatically. This can include software tools such as revision control systems, content management systems, and document management systems. Versioning can be useful for many different types of documents, such as source code, technical documents, design documents, or research papers, and it is important in many fields such as software development, engineering, and academic research. It helps to track the changes, collaborate on the document, and have a consistent version of the document.

Document versioning allows you to keep track of changes made to a document over time, storing each version separately. This makes it easy to see who made what changes and when, as well as to roll back to previous versions if necessary. During a merger or acquisition, document versioning can be particularly useful in several ways:

Maintaining clarity and transparency: Mergers and acquisitions require a high level of communication and coordination between parties. By using document versioning, everyone involved can stay on the same page and always know where the document stands.

Facilitating due diligence: During the due diligence process, both parties will need to scrutinize many documents closely. Document versioning provides an efficient and streamlined process for keeping track of the changes and ensuring that everyone has access to the latest version.

Preserving institutional knowledge: During a merger or acquisition, employees may come and go, but institutional knowledge is vital. By using document versioning, businesses can ensure that vital information is preserved, even if key personnel leave the organization. Some common types of documents that benefit from version control during mergers and acquisitions are contracts, non-disclosure agreements, intellectual property documentation, financial statements, legal documents, and employee information.

Document versioning ensures transparency and provides an efficient way to manage and track changes in a vast array of documents.

Document redlining

Document redlining means that a tool offers markup of changes done in a document. When one user changes sections of the document, these sections are marked up in colors, and it is documented who did such marked up change in the document.

Here's how document redlining can benefit your company during the M&A process.

Clarity of Changes Made: By using document redlining, the specific changes made to an existing document are much clearer to both parties involved in the negotiation process. This clarity helps to avoid any misunderstandings, uncertainties, and delays that may arise during the negotiations process.

Improved Efficiency: Document redlining helps to speed up the M&A process by allowing both parties to quickly review and respond to proposed changes rather than spending time identifying them. The use of redlining documents makes it much easier for both parties to quickly identify areas of agreement and disagreement, which helps to streamline the negotiation process.

Reduced Risks: Using document redlining ensures that all changes made to existing documents are tracked and can be reviewed and approved by all parties involved in the M&A process. This helps to reduce the risk of mistakes, oversights, and misunderstandings leading to legal or operational issues in the future.

Enhanced Negotiation: Document redlining helps to create transparency between the parties involved, leading to enhanced negotiation processes. By both parties being aware of each other's proposed changes, they can approach the document's negotiation from a more informed, conciliatory perspective. This helps to avoid any confrontation and ensures that both parties can reach an agreement that is mutually beneficial.

In conclusion, merger and acquisition transactions are a costly and time-consuming process. Document redlining can be an effective tool for managing this process, minimizing risks, and ensuring that the final agreement is fair and transparent to all parties involved. By using document redlining during M&A transactions, companies can ensure a more effective negotiations process and higher chances of reaching an agreement.

Watermarking

Watermarking is the process of embedding information, such as a logo, text or a digital signature, into a digital image, audio, or video. The resulting watermarks can be visible or invisible. This technique is used to assert ownership and identify the origin of digital content, and to prevent unauthorized use or distribution of the content. Watermarking can be done using various techniques, such as visible watermarks, invisible watermarks, and digital signatures, and can be applied to various types of digital media, including images, audio and video files.

Watermarking is widely used in fields such as digital rights management, broadcasting, and publishing to protect the rights of the creator and owners. Watermarking can be used to establish an audit trail.

By incorporating watermarks into important documents, companies can ensure that their assets are properly protected during mergers and acquisitions. There are several ways to use watermarking for M&A.

The first is to use watermarks on sensitive or confidential documents. By adding a watermark that indicates that the document is confidential, or company property, organizations and employees can be reminded to handle it with care. This ensures that sensitive information is not leaked or mishandled during the merger or acquisition process. Another way to use watermarking is to add a watermark to intellectual property, such as logos or product designs, that clearly identifies ownership or origin. This makes it easier to track and prove ownership and protect against infringement. Finally, watermarking can also be used to monitor and track the distribution of documents and intellectual property during the merger or acquisition process. By including unique watermarks on each copy of a document or image, organizations can track who is accessing and using the information and ensure that it is being used in accordance with the terms of the merger or acquisition agreement.

Using visible or invisible watermarks on sensitive documents and intellectual property can help to ensure that they are not leaked, mishandled, or infringed upon. In addition, by tracking the distribution and use of these assets through watermarking, companies can ensure that their assets are being used in accordance with the terms of the merger or acquisition agreement.

Integration technology

A seamless experience between tasks

Seamless experience is the requirement to execute several tasks without having to switch between different tools. Imagine conducting a technical due diligence of a software product without switching tools.

Seamless integration with other tools

Seamless integration means that there is no manual intervention needed if a switch between tasks also means a switch between tools.

With advancements in technology, it is no longer necessary to manually input data into multiple systems. By using tools that integrate seamlessly, companies can share information across platforms, reducing error rates and increasing overall efficiency.

Seamless integration can also provide a more consistent user experience, which can be essential during times of change. By connecting tools such as HR and payroll software, employees can gain access to all relevant information. This ensures that they are paid correctly, have access to benefits, and understand how organizational changes may impact them. In summary, leveraging seamless integration between tools is essential for organizations going through mergers and acquisitions.

Data integration features

Data integration is the ability of a tool to integrate data from various data sources and applications. An example is the use of data from the internet or a database of the buyer company within a tool. Another example is the integration of data from a data room into a tool for contract reviews of another vendor.

Machine learning technology

Machine learning technology is often used in combination with analytics, natural language processing and document processing. This is why we only have two technologies listed here and other uses can be found in the sections for analytics, natural language processing or document processing.

Other applications of machine learning

This attribute collects all other ways to use machine learning in tools which are not covered by the other machine learning attributes described here. One example would be graph encoders, which is machine learning based on annotated graphs.

While some applications of machine learning in M&A such as market analysis, customer profiling, and risk assessment are widely known, there are other unique ways in which machine learning can be utilized. Here are some other applications of machine learning that can be used during mergers and acquisitions:

Contract Review Automation: Contract review is a tedious and time-consuming process. With the help of machine learning, companies can use Natural Language Processing (NLP) algorithms to analyze and extract relevant information from contracts.

Predictive Analytics/Modeling: Machine learning can help in creating predictive models based on historical data from the companies involved in mergers or acquisitions. This can help to predict the performance of the merged or acquired company in the future.

Fraud Detection: Machine learning algorithms can be used to detect fraudulent activities during mergers and acquisitions. By analyzing financial and operational data, machine learning algorithms can identify patterns and anomalies that can indicate fraud.

Customer Churn Prediction: Acquiring a company with a large customer base is beneficial, but what if those customers start churning after the merger or acquisition? Machine learning algorithms can help in predicting customer churn and finding ways to prevent it.

Cultural Compatibility Analysis: Merging two companies means bringing their employees together. Machine learning algorithms can be used to analyze the cultural differences between companies to ensure a smooth integration process. In conclusion, using machine learning in mergers and acquisitions can help companies make informed decisions that can lead to successful outcomes.

By utilizing some of the less known applications of machine learning such as contract review automation, predictive modeling, fraud detection, customer churn prediction, and cultural compatibility analysis, companies can maximize the benefits of machine learning in M&A.

Knowledge graphs

A knowledge graph is a data structure that represents entities (such as people, places, and things) and the relationships between them. It is a graphical representation of knowledge, where entities are represented as nodes and their relationships as edges. Knowledge graphs are used to organize and structure large and complex sets of information, making it easier to understand and navigate. They are often used in natural language processing, semantic web, and artificial intelligence applications. A knowledge graph can be used to represent different types of knowledge, such as facts, rules, and concepts. They can also be used to represent different types of relationships between entities, such as is-a, part-of, and has-a. They can be used to power search engines, semantic search, chatbots, question answering systems, and other applications that need to understand the meaning of natural language text.

Knowledge graphs have received a lot of attention lately, and with good reason. For M&A, knowledge graphs can provide a comprehensive, holistic view of relevant data, relationships, and insights to inform decision-making throughout the M&A process.

Let's take a closer look at some of the ways knowledge graphs can be used for M&A. Firstly, knowledge graphs can assist in the due diligence process by providing a structured way to organize and analyze business data. With a knowledge graph, companies can extract, organize, and connect critical information from various sources such as financial statements, contracts, legal documents, and communication records. By identifying and mapping the relationships between data points, knowledge graphs can enable deeper analysis and uncover potential risks and opportunities that might otherwise remain hidden.

Secondly, knowledge graphs can enhance post-merger integration efforts by providing a unified view of the acquired company operations and systems, as well as identifying overlaps and potential synergies. This is especially important in cases where there may be different operating models, systems, and processes between the merging companies. Knowledge graphs can facilitate the integration process by identifying redundancies, gaps, and areas for collaboration or consolidation.

Finally, knowledge graphs can provide a foundation for ongoing insights and analytics post-merger. With a comprehensive view of merged data, knowledge graphs can track and monitor performance metrics, support data-driven decision-making, and evaluate the effectiveness of integration efforts. In conclusion, knowledge graphs bring a new level of clarity and structure to M&A efforts. Whether it's streamlining due diligence, improving post-merger integration, or providing ongoing insights, knowledge graphs can enable companies to make informed decisions with greater speed and accuracy.

Natural language processing technology

Automated redaction

Automatic redaction is the process of automatically obscuring or removing sensitive or confidential information from a document. This is typically done using software tools that are programmed to recognize specific types of information, such as personal identification numbers, financial data, or trade secrets, and obscure or remove them from the document. Redaction is often used to protect sensitive information from being disclosed to unauthorized individuals or to comply with legal requirements for protecting the privacy of certain types of data.

During M&A, automated redaction can assist with due diligence by quickly processing large volumes of documents and highlighting areas that need redaction. This efficiency can significantly reduce the errors and omissions that can result from manual redaction, ensuring a more comprehensive and accurate document set.

Another benefit of automated redaction is improved data security. Sensitive information is no longer left exposed during the sharing of documents between parties, reducing the risk of data breaches and compliance violations.

Companies can also efficiently enforce document retention policies with automated redaction, ensuring that all irrelevant information is removed from documents before storage.

While there are many benefits of automated redaction, it is essential to note that this technology is not a fully automated solution for redaction. Companies still need to carefully review documents after redaction to ensure the accuracy of the redacted information. Additionally, automated redaction does not replace the need for legal expertise during M&A.

In conclusion, automated redaction is a valuable tool for companies looking to streamline their M&A processes while improving data security. With its efficiency and precision, it not only reduces the workload but also reduces the risk of errors, oversights, and compliance failures.

Automatic translation

Automated translation, also known as machine translation, is the process of translating text or speech from one language to another using a computer program. Automated translation is fast and can handle a large volume of text, but the quality of the translations may not be as high as those produced by a human translator. This is a feature that can be used if a target does business in different countries that need contracts to be signed in different languages by country.

One challenge that arises during M&A processes is the language barrier, particularly when dealing with companies from different regions or countries.

The use of automatic translation tools has been steadily increasing in recent years, and for good reasons. These tools can quickly and accurately translate large quantities of text, making them invaluable for companies involved in mergers and acquisitions.

One-way automatic translation can be used during mergers and acquisitions is for due diligence. During this stage, companies need to review and analyze a vast array of documents, including legal contracts, financial statements, and employee agreements. With automatic translation, these documents can be quickly translated into the desired language, allowing for faster and more efficient due diligence.

Another area where automatic translation can be useful is communication between parties. When negotiating the terms of a merger or acquisition, there may be language barriers that can slow down or complicate the process. Using automatic translation, businesses can easily communicate with one another, ensuring that negotiations run smoothly and are not hindered by language barriers. It's worth noting that while automatic translation tools are incredibly helpful, they should not be relied on exclusively. These tools are not perfect and may make errors, particularly when dealing with colloquial language or technical jargon. It's important to have a human translator review important documents to ensure accuracy and avoid misunderstandings.

In conclusion, automatic translation can be an asset for companies involved in mergers and acquisitions. By streamlining communication and simplifying due diligence, these tools can help businesses complete transactions more efficiently and effectively.

Automatic summarization

If the content of several original documents can be converted into one document and the resulting document is shorter than the sum of the original documents, we call this summarization. We call it automatic summarization if this summarization is happening in a fully automated fashion. An example is the automated creation of a contract based on a historic contract document and many amendments. The changes to the historic contract document documented by the amendments are automatically applied to the historic document to create a new contract document containing all the changes. Automated summarization is a natural language processing task that involves generating a concise and fluent summary of a longer document or collection of documents. The goal of automated summarization is to produce a summary that conveys the most important information in the original document, while preserving its meaning and style.

While you must deal with large amounts of information, distilling the most critical data points to make decisions can be a daunting task. This is where automatic summarization comes in. Automatic summarization is a powerful tool that helps organizations deal with incoming information in real-time.

The primary benefit of automatic summarization is that it makes the decision-making process faster and smarter. It transforms raw data into easily digestible summaries, allowing decision-makers to focus on the most crucial data points. By doing so, decision-makers can arrive at informed decisions that lead to positive outcomes.

Automatic summarization also helps to preserve data quality. By leveraging automatic summarization tools, organizations can quickly identify inconsistencies in data or errors that could otherwise go unnoticed. This is essential for ensuring that the data used in decision-making is accurate, timely, and consistent.

Another benefit of automatic summarization is its ability to improve collaboration and communication. By automating the task of summarizing documents, organizations can significantly reduce the time and resources required to process these documents to extract valuable insights.

Speech recognition

Speech recognition is the process of converting spoken words into written or machine-readable text. This technology uses algorithms and machine learning techniques to analyze and interpret human speech and can be used for a variety of applications such as voice commands, dictation, and transcription. This technology is widely used in fields such as speech-to-text, voice command, voice-controlled devices, and natural language processing. Examples are Apple´s Siri and Amazon´s Alexa, which recognize speech to determine tasks to be executed.

One of the main benefits of utilizing speech recognition in M&A is the speed at which information can be processed. Instead of having to manually type out notes or transcribe meetings, speech recognition software can quickly and accurately capture spoken conversations. This can lead to a faster turnaround time for due diligence and expedite the overall process of closing the transaction.

Another benefit is increased accuracy. Typing can be prone to human error, especially if notes are being taken during a fast-paced meeting. With speech recognition, the software can accurately capture each spoken word and take note of important details that may have been missed during manual transcription. This can lead to more comprehensive and detailed notes that can improve decision-making during the due diligence process.

Moreover, speech recognition technology can also provide more security during M&A transactions. Traditionally, hand-written notes and documentation can be easily misplaced or shared without proper authorization. However, speech recognition software can offer various levels of security to ensure that sensitive information is only accessible to authorized parties.

In conclusion, speech recognition technology can make M&A transactions more efficient, accurate, and secure.

Speech generation

Speech generation, also known as text-to-speech (TTS), is the process of converting written or machine-readable text into spoken words. This technology uses algorithms and machine learning techniques to generate speech that sounds like a human voice. Speech generation systems can be divided into two main categories: rule-based and statistical. Rule-based systems use a set of predefined rules to generate speech, while statistical systems use machine learning techniques to model the patterns and variations of human speech.

One way speech generation technology can enhance M&A is by providing real-time translation of languages. In a global marketplace, where businesses are no longer confined to their native countries, M&As can involve parties that speak different languages. Speech generation technology can translate discussions and negotiations in real-time, facilitating open communication and reducing the possibility of misunderstandings that could hinder the M&A process.

Another way speech generation technology is to aid M&As is through audible meeting transcriptions. Meetings can be transcribed into text and analyzed quickly, highlighting critical topics of interest for parties. This makes it easier for all parties to stay informed and ensures that everyone is on the same page. By cutting down on miscommunication and enabling faster decision-making, parties can close M&A deals more efficiently using speech-to-text software technologies.

Speech generation technology can also enhance M&A negotiations by examining the tone of voices. During negotiations, tone can shape the direction of discussions. Speech-to-text software technologies now optimize voice recognition algorithms to capture the tone of the speaker, enabling other parties to determine if the speaker is comfortable with the direction of the negotiation or if there is a problem that needs to be addressed. This information supports the negotiation process to keep both parties happy with the outcome.

Finally, speech generation technology can facilitate post-closing integration by providing audio feedback to employees. For instance, audio streams can be used to deliver important training or updates to staff members of acquired companies. These audio streams are more engaging than traditional presentations, and users can listen at their own pace, covering some instances or topics several times to consolidate the message. In conclusion, speech generation technology is proving to be a valuable tool in M&A processes.

Semantic interpretation of data

Semantic interpretation means that data, e.g., pictures or strings or numbers, automatically get a semantic meaning assigned. One example could be that a tool recognizes if a document is a contract or if a number is a revenue number.

Here are some ways semantic interpretation of data can be used during these transactions:

Identify areas of overlap: By analyzing the data, businesses can quickly identify areas where both companies have similar offerings or capabilities. By recognizing these overlaps, businesses can determine which areas are most valuable and where resources should be dedicated.

Determine cultural alignment: Semantic interpretation of data can be used to evaluate the cultural fit between two companies. By analyzing the data, businesses can determine the values and beliefs of each company and identify where there may be alignment or misalignment. Knowing the cultural fit between companies can help during integration efforts.

Assess risks: During mergers and acquisitions, businesses must evaluate potential risks associated with the transaction. Semantic interpretation can help identify potential red flags within the data, such as non-compliance with regulations or financial irregularities. By identifying these issues early on, businesses can take steps to address them before they become bigger problems.

Improve communication: Misunderstandings and miscommunications are common during mergers and acquisitions. Semantic interpretation can help facilitate clear communication by ensuring that everyone involved in the transaction understands the meaning behind the language used. This approach can help reduce misunderstandings and the likelihood of conflicts.

In conclusion, semantic interpretation of data is an invaluable tool for businesses involved in mergers and acquisitions. It can help increase efficiency, improve communication, and reduce risks associated with the transaction.

Disambiguation

Disambiguation refers to the process of resolving ambiguity in language or text. In the context of natural language processing or information retrieval, disambiguation is the task of identifying the intended meaning of a word or phrase in a given context. This is often necessary because many words have multiple meanings or can be used in different ways, making it difficult to understand the intended meaning of a text or speech.

Automatic disambiguation uses algorithms to identify and eliminate ambiguity in data, thereby ensuring that the data is consistent and coherent. Such disambiguation can be performed using various techniques, such as statistical methods, machine learning, or rule-based methods.

One of the main goals of disambiguation is to improve the precision and recall of information retrieval systems and natural language processing applications, by identifying the correct meaning of a term. It is also an important task in many applications such as speech recognition, machine translation, and automatic summarization.

Disambiguation is a critical tool in the M&A process that can help companies avoid confusion and ensure that all stakeholders are on the same page. This can involve identifying multiple meanings or interpretations of terms and concepts that are commonly used in the industry.

Search function

If you can search for a sequence of words and find them in different documents, this is called simple phrase search. An example is searching for the phrase 'warranty' and finding documents that contain the exact word 'warranty'.

Semantic search

Semantic search allows to search data based on their semantic interpretation. An example is searching for a limitation of warranty clause and any clause representing a limitation of warranty is found. Or searching for all information related to a specific customer, which would show customer revenues, customer contracts and any information about the interaction of the target company with a customer.

Here are some ways that organizations can leverage Semantic Search to support their merging efforts:

Efficient Data Collection: Before engaging in a merger or acquisition process, organizations need to gather a large amount of data about both companies involved. With Semantic Search, you can easily extract relevant data from both internal and external sources, and search for information by using natural language queries. This allows organizations to efficiently collect data, which leads to better decision-making during the merging process.

Improved Market Intelligence: Semantic Search can help organizations gain insights into market trends and potential opportunities, which in turn can help inform business decisions. By analyzing both structured and unstructured data, Semantic Search can help uncover trends and patterns that might be difficult to identify using traditional methods.

Efficient Due Diligence: Due diligence is the process of investigating and assessing the financial and legal aspects of a company before a merger or acquisition. Semantic Search can help organizations efficiently review many documents and identify key information that may be relevant to the due diligence process. By using natural language queries and machine learning algorithms, Semantic Search can automatically pinpoint critical areas for due diligence, helping organizations make informed decisions.

Enhanced Collaboration: Semantic Search can help improve collaboration between teams involved in mergers and acquisitions. By providing a single platform to access and analyze data, Semantic Search can help teams communicate and collaborate more effectively. This can help speed up decision making and increase efficiency during the process.

Overall, semantic search has emerged as a critical tool for organizations looking to streamline and improve their merging process. By leveraging its capabilities, organizations can gain valuable insights from vast amounts of data, conduct efficient due diligence, and enhance collaboration between teams involved in mergers and acquisitions.

Forensic search

Forensic search allows us to traverse existing databases and collections of electronic documents based on semantic relationships between entities contained in documents or data. An example is 'any information in the data room regarding the customer company Bosch', which is expected to find customer contracts, customer service information etc. and to show semantic relationships with the customer Bosch.

Forensic search techniques can also be useful in M&A investigations by uncovering hidden or undisclosed information that could impact the value of the deal. Here are some ways to utilize forensic search during M&As:

Identify and validate financial information: Forensic search can be used to verify financial information provided by the target company, such as revenue, expenses, and cash flow. By analyzing electronic data such as financial statements, bank statements, and accounting records, forensic search can identify any irregularities, anomalies, or signs of fraud. This can help avoid significant financial losses, reputational damage, and legal liabilities that could arise from undisclosed financial issues.

Uncover hidden assets or liabilities: During M&A investigations, companies need to identify any undisclosed assets or liabilities that could have a significant effect on the value of the deal. Forensic search can help identify hidden assets or liabilities by analyzing electronic data such as company emails, documents, and financial records. This can help ensure that all assets and liabilities are accounted for and that the value of the deal is accurate.

Protect against legal liability: During M&A investigations, companies need to ensure that they are not exposed to any legal liability associated with the target company. Forensic research can help identify potential legal risks by analyzing electronic data such as litigation files, contractual agreements, and regulatory compliance records. This can help protect the company from unforeseen legal liabilities and minimize potential financial losses.

Forensic search can be a valuable tool for companies involved in M&A investigations. By using forensic search techniques, companies can verify financial information, uncover hidden assets or liabilities, and protect against legal liabilities.

Multi-language capabilities

Multi-language capability is the feature of a tool to provide a UI and functionality in different languages. This can be used if, within and M&A project, users need UIs in different languages or other functionality in different languages like natural language processing, automatic summarization, or automatic translation.

So, how can you use multi-language capabilities during mergers and acquisitions? Firstly, it is essential to understand the languages spoken by employees, clients, and stakeholders involved in the merger or acquisition. This information will help you determine the appropriate strategy for communication and collaboration throughout the process.

Secondly, having access to professional translation and interpretation services can bridge language gaps and facilitate smooth communication between parties. These services can include legal and financial documents, as well as verbal communication during important meetings.

Lastly, utilizing specialized software such as language learning apps, translation software, and real-time interpretation services can also help companies optimize multi-language capabilities during mergers and acquisitions.

In conclusion, the success of mergers and acquisitions heavily relies on effective communication and collaboration between all parties involved. By utilizing multi-language capabilities, companies can ensure successful M&A processes and strengthen their position in a multinational marketplace.

Process automation technology

Robotic process automation

Robotic process automation (RPA) is a type of technology that allows software robots, or "bots," to automate repetitive, routine tasks that are typically performed by humans. This technology can be used to automate tasks such as data entry, form filling, and data processing, as well as more complex tasks such as invoice processing and customer service interactions. RPA is typically implemented by using a software bot to interact with the user interface of an existing application, mimicking the actions of a human user. The software bot can be programmed to follow a set of rules or instructions to perform a specific task or set of tasks and can be integrated with other systems and applications to automate end-to-end processes. RPA can significantly improve process efficiency, reduce the risk of errors, and free up employees to focus on higher-value tasks.

In the context of M&A, RPA can be used to automate tasks such as data entry, contract review, and compliance checks. For example, a software robot can be trained to extract data from financial statements and perform a financial analysis, saving human analysts time and effort.

Similarly, a robot can be used to review contracts and identify any discrepancies or legal risks, reducing the need for lawyers to manually review each document. Another area where RPA can be useful is in managing the integration of two companies after a merger.

Often, the process of integrating two different IT systems, HR processes, and invoice systems can be challenging and time-consuming. RPA can help by automating some of these integration tasks and ensuring that data is transferred accurately and efficiently. This can also help to reduce the risk of errors and ensure that the new organization is up and running as quickly as possible.

RPA is not a one-size-fits-all solution, and its effectiveness in automating M&A processes will depend on factors such as the size of the deal, the complexity of the tasks involved, and the level of standardization of processes. However, for companies that are looking to streamline their M&A processes and reduce manual effort, RPA can be a powerful tool.

Security technology

Secure file viewer

To avoid data loss or leakage, a secure file viewer traces and logs access to data and documents and keeps them safe. Imagine taking data from the due diligence phase to the next phase automatically.

Here are some ways in which you can use a secure file viewer during M&A:

Share files securely: During an M&A, you will need to share a lot of files with various parties, including lawyers, accountants, and potential buyers. A secure file viewer allows you to share these files without the risk of them being intercepted or stolen. You can also track who has accessed the files and when, giving you greater control over the due diligence process.

View files without downloading: With a secure file viewer, you can view files without downloading them. This is important because it reduces the risk of the files being saved or distributed without your permission. It also saves time and storage space, as you don't need to download multiple copies of the same file.

Restrict access to sensitive files: During an M&A, you may have files that contain highly sensitive information, such as financial statements or intellectual property. In such cases, you can use a secure file viewer to restrict access to these files. You can set permissions so that only certain people can view or download the files, and you can track who has accessed them.

Security audit trail

A security audit trail exists if a tool records all security-relevant activities and provides the sequence of such activities together with the information on who did what and when.

As companies go through mergers and acquisitions (M&A), it is essential to ensure that the sensitive data and information involved in the process remain secure. This is where the use of security audit trail becomes relevant.

A security audit trail is a feature that allows businesses to monitor and track all user activity within their system. This includes actions such as logins, file access, modifications to data, and more. With security audit trails in place, companies can better manage the risks of data breaches and ensure that any suspicious activities are detected and addressed promptly.

During M&A, the security audit trail feature becomes even more critical. It helps the companies involved to analyze user activity on both sides to ensure that no unauthorized access or transfers take place. This is especially important as sensitive data may need to be shared between the merging companies' systems, and it is crucial to ensure that this is done securely. In addition to enhancing security measures, audit trails can also be used as evidence in case of disputes that may arise during the M&A process.

In the event of a breach or data leak, the audit trail can help pinpoint the source of the issue, the affected assets, and the individuals involved. To make the most of security audit trails during M&A, businesses should ensure that they have access to accurate and up-to-date information.

They should also ensure that all activity on the system is properly monitored, recorded, and audited. Finally, all staff involved in the process should be trained on the importance of security audit trails and have a clear understanding of what is expected of them.

Using security audit trails is an essential measure for any company, especially during M&A transactions. Not only does it enhance security and reduce the risk of data breaches, but it also provides a mechanism for tracking events and addressing any issues that may arise. Therefore, it is crucial to implement robust security audit trail features to ensure that companies can effectively navigate through M&A transactions while keeping their data and information secure.

Data security

Data security refers to the set of practices and measures that are implemented to protect sensitive and confidential information from unauthorized access, use, disclosure, disruption, modification, or destruction. This can include measures such as encryption, access controls, firewalls, and intrusion detection systems, as well as policies and procedures for managing and protecting data throughout its lifecycle. Additionally, data security may include incident response and disaster recovery planning, regular security audits and testing, and employee training on security best practices. The goal of data security is to ensure confidentiality, integrity, and availability of sensitive information, and to prevent data breaches and other security incidents that can harm organizations and individuals. Here are ways to use automated data security during mergers and acquisitions:

Conduct A Data Inventory: Before finalizing any agreement, conduct a data inventory audit that covers all data, including customer data and financial reports. Determine what data you will keep or destroy based on relevance and privacy laws.

Monitor All Data Migration Processes: Data migration is an essential stage in the merger and requires tight data security. Ensure that all data is encrypted, and access is limited only to authorized personnel.

Data privacy and protection

Privacy and data protection laws in different countries enforce certain rules regarding the access to and the protection of personal identifiable information. The impact of these laws is summarized using the term data privacy and data protection. A tool supports data privacy and protection if it fulfills or helps the user to fulfill requirements for data privacy and protection.

Sole access in EU countries

EU access means that data are stored within the European union and only tool vendor personnel located in the EU has access to the data. This can be a requirement from companies operating within the European Union.

Education and training content and technology

Playbooks

Playbooks are predefined documents that tell how tasks are executed. They often include step-by-step instructions. For example, a Playbook could describe the tasks and templates used to conduct due diligence. Playbooks should be provided by the tools you use to automate the process as always-on reference. Here are some ways you can use playbooks to ensure a successful merger or acquisition:

Defining the Scope: Playbooks provide a holistic view of the merger or acquisition. By defining the scope and objectives of the transaction, you can align and focus on the activities towards achieving those goals.

Identifying Risks: Playbooks allow you to identify potential risks and challenges that could arise during the transaction. Once identified, you can create plans to mitigate those risks and minimize their impact on the transaction.

Assigning Tasks: Playbooks provide a centralized location where you can assign and track tasks. Assigning specific tasks to team members ensures everyone knows what they need to do and when, eliminating confusion and misunderstandings.

Managing Communication: Effective communication is crucial during mergers and acquisitions. Playbooks provide a platform for team members to communicate and collaborate quickly and easily, allowing for efficient decision-making and problem-solving.

Documenting the Process: Playbooks provide a trail of documentation that captures the activities and decisions made during the transaction. This documentation is valuable for future reference and can be used to evaluate the success of the transaction.

In conclusion, using playbooks can help you navigate the complexities involved in mergers and acquisitions.

Sample content

Sample content are documents relating to the task at hand and show exemplary results. Tools should provide such sample content to the users. One of the primary benefits of using sample content in mergers and acquisitions is that it can help streamline the process. Sample content can provide a starting point for the development of legal agreements, contracts, and other essential documents. Having sample content readily available can save time and resources that would otherwise be spent creating these documents from scratch.

Additionally, sample content can help ensure consistency in the documentation process, which is important during a merger or acquisition when multiple parties are involved.

Another advantage of using sample content during mergers and acquisitions is that it can facilitate due diligence. Sample content can be used to provide a framework for due diligence, including financial statements, market research, and other information. This information can help investors and stakeholders make informed decisions about the potential risks and benefits of an investment.

Finally, sample content can play a critical role in the integration process following a merger or acquisition. By having sample content for policies, procedures, and other internal documentation, both parties can ensure a smooth transition. Sample content can help ensure consistency and clarity in communication, which is essential when different organizational cultures are merging into one.

Task-specific questions or questionnaires

The questions are requests for information needed to fulfill the task at hand. Questions are often listed in sequence as questionnaires.

Here are some reasons why task-specific questions are so valuable in M&A:

When it comes to mergers and acquisitions, time is of the essence. The longer the process takes, the more it can cost both financially and in terms of employee morale. By asking task-specific questions at the outset, you can identify potential problems and address them quickly. This can help keep the process moving smoothly and avoid costly delays.

The due diligence process typically involves multiple teams, from finance to HR to legal. Each team has its own set of responsibilities and expertise. By asking task-specific questions, you can ensure that everyone is on the same page and working toward the same goal. They can help simplify complex tasks and allow employees to focus on tasks that require their specific skills.

The due diligence process is all about identifying potential risks and mitigating them. By asking task-specific questions, you can identify areas of concern and take steps to reduce or eliminate any risks. This can include everything from legal issues to financial red flags.

The use of task-specific questions can help make the process smoother, reduce risks, and improve communication between teams.

Real-life examples

Real life examples are content relating to a task that comes from practitioners and report about experiences in executing the task in real M&A projects.

Real-life examples can serve as references for stakeholders and help them understand the practical implications of decisions made during the M&A process. The following are some ways to use real-life examples during an M&A:

Identify Successful M&A Use Cases: One way to incorporate real-life examples is by identifying successful M&A cases in the same or similar industries. These use cases can serve as a reference point and provide insights into how other companies navigated the M&A process. Analyzing the strategies that worked for them can help stakeholders align their goals and expectations for the M&A.

Use Case Studies: Case studies are effective tools for learning from real-life examples. Companies can use case studies to illustrate how M&A can create value. Additionally, case studies can give stakeholders insights on how to manage various aspects of the M&A, such as cultural differences among organizations, communication challenges, and post-merger integration planning.

Leverage Stories from Previous M&A Experience: M&A teams can share stories about previous deals they were involved in, focusing on successes and challenges they faced during the process. These stories can help stakeholders understand what to expect in the M&A process and can help them better prepare for the challenges that lie ahead.

Create a Repository of Best Practices: Companies can build an internal repository of M&A best practices, incorporating real-life examples. This repository can include case studies, playbooks, and checklists that M&A teams can use to execute M&A deals successfully. Regular updates on this repository can help ensure it remains relevant and useful. In conclusion, incorporating real-life examples throughout the M&A process is key to achieving a successful deal. Real-life examples help stakeholders understand the practical implications of decisions made during the M&A process and provide insights into how to navigate the complexities of a deal. By identifying successful M&A use cases, leveraging case studies, sharing previous M&A experience, and creating a repository of best practices, companies can increase the probability of a successful M&A.

Articles

Articles are excerpts from books, blogs or other publications related to the the task at hand, the execution of the task or the subject matter. Articles can help the person carrying out the task to do a better job.

Task-specific training

Task training is content provided to enable the user to execute the task at hand, independent of tools.

Task-specific training is a crucial tool that can help in facilitating a smooth transition for both the existing and newly hired employees. The key benefits of task-specific training for mergers and acquisitions are:

Increase in Productivity - By providing task-specific training, employees can develop the skills needed to perform their job duties effectively. This can lead to an increase in productivity, as they will be able to complete their tasks in a shorter amount of time.

Consistency in Processes - It is crucial to establish consistency in processes across the newly merged or acquired organization. Task-specific training helps to ensure that all employees are trained on the same processes, reducing the risk of errors or inefficiencies.

Reduction in Turnover - Employees who receive effective job training are more likely to stay with the organization. This translates into reduced turnover rates, which can save the organization time, and resources in the long run.

Improved Customer Satisfaction - Customers of the newly merged or acquired organization expect quality service from day one. Task-specific training will equip employees with the knowledge and skills to provide the level of service that customers expect. To develop and implement effective task-specific training, companies must first identify the exact tasks, and skill sets employees will require in the new organization. This can be achieved through a comprehensive needs analysis. Once the training needs are identified, a tailored training program can be developed for each employee. The training program should include hands-on exercises, interactive learning modules, and opportunities for feedback and assessment. In conclusion, the key to a successful merger or acquisition is the integration of employees into the new organization. Task-specific training is a vital tool that can make the transition smooth and seamless. With proper planning and execution, companies can ensure that their employees are fully equipped to perform their job duties effectively, resulting in improved productivity, consistency in processes, reduced turnover, and improved customer satisfaction.

Tool-specific training

Tool training is content provided to enable the user to execute the task with the use of a specific tool.

Investing in tool-specific training can provide numerous benefits during M&A processes. By ensuring that all employees are proficient in the tools and software systems being used, businesses can avoid unnecessary delays and disruptions. Additionally, training can improve employee confidence and productivity, ultimately leading to improved overall performance. Before undergoing an M&A transaction, companies should analyze which tools and software systems will be necessary for effective integration. Then, a training program can be designed to help employees familiarize themselves with the specific tools and software systems being used post-acquisition. This should be done as early as possible in the M&A process to ensure all employees are prepared for the changes that will be implemented. The benefits of tool-specific training are countless. Employees will be better equipped to handle their tasks and responsibilities, resulting in more efficient processes and increased job satisfaction. Trained employees will also be more adaptable to new processes and tools, ensuring a smoother transition during the M&A process. In conclusion, investing in tool-specific training during mergers and acquisitions is a smart move for businesses. Proper training will ensure that all employees are prepared for the changes that will take place and can handle any challenges that come their way.

Agent Technology

Software agent technology

Distributed multi-agent technology refers to systems that consist of multiple agents (autonomous software entities that can act on their own) that are distributed across a network and are able to communicate with each other in order to achieve a common goal. These systems can be used in a variety of applications, including distributed problem solving, distributed decision making, and distributed control. They are often used in scenarios where it is necessary to coordinate the actions of multiple agents to achieve a desired outcome.

Software agents based on agentic AI are massively assisting experts and take up most of the workload for merger integration. View software agents as subject matter experts and coworkers, not pieces of software. They assist in data collection and the processing of the data along the steps in the integration process.

2.4   Data for the M&A process

Mergers and acquisitions (M&A) signify complicated transactions that demand detailed assessment and knowledgeable choices. Central to this undertaking are the data sources that deliver vital information and insights needed to assess prospective deals. Below is a summary of key data sources commonly utilized in the M&A process.

Company Data about the buyer

This seems obvious, but often the data about the buyer are just included in Powerpoint slides and the amount of data are limited. Strategy formulation ends up in sentences but cannot be used in an automated fashion. Also, detailed data relating to the buyer's organizational structure, sales operations, partnerships, customer base etc. are not used to its full extent. Our goal is to use all available data about the buyer to determine the impact of the acquisition, like e.g. how much of the acquired products can be sold via sales channels of the buyer or to determine consolidation effects in the supply chain of the buyer and target company.

Company Data about the target

Company data is integral for comprehending the operational, financial, and strategic standing of an entity under consideration. It supports the execution of meticulous research, analyzing threats, and correctly estimating the company's value. Dependable company data guarantees that decisions are based on sound information, thereby increasing the probability of a successful merger or acquisition.

Bloomberg and Refinitiv serve as leading purveyors of financial data encompassing   corporate   earnings,   stock   market   performance, comprehensive market analysis, and additional relevant information. These resources contribute significantly to the development of a sophisticated understanding of the financial environment that influences prospective targets.

Corporations that are publicly traded are mandated to publish financial statements and other critical documents, which are obtainable via the SEC's EDGAR database in the United States or through analogous institutions globally. Such data is instrumental in facilitating comparisons between potential targets and industry standards.

Although less readily available than public information, data pertaining to private companies can be acquired through platforms dedicated to insights on private enterprises, such as Preqin or CB Insights. These platforms yield valuable information regarding private company valuations, investment funding, and operational performance.

But there are new collections of data, which were opaque before, that are used by disruptive tools like ABRAMS world trade wiki. In this case, it is detailed information about the supply chains and chains of customers of target companies.

Market Data

Market data is instrumental in recognizing trends and market dynamics that affect the valuation and prospects of a target company. It bolsters strategic planning by pinpointing opportunities and threats within the market, thus guiding investment decisions.

Supply Chain Data

Supply chain data is essential for detecting potential synergies or inefficiencies within the integrated operations. Proactively addressing supply chain issues can result in more seamless integration with minimal disruptions, thereby ensuring operational continuity following the merger.

Intellectual Property Data

Intellectual property data is pivotal in assessing a company's competitive advantage, particularly within technology and innovation-centric sectors. It is critical for ascertaining the intrinsic worth of the company and safeguarding its fundamental assets.

Go-To-Market Data

Go-to-market data guarantees that the merged entities synchronize their sales strategies and branding effectively to forge a cohesive market presence. It is instrumental in preserving client relationships and maintaining market standing throughout the transition.

In conclusion, the proficient application of various data sources is imperative within the context of mergers and acquisitions. These data sources not only furnish the essential empirical evidence requisite for assessment but also equip stakeholders with the critical insights necessary for making judicious decisions. As technological advancements progress, the capacity to analyze and integrate data swiftly and precisely will perpetually influence the execution beyond M&A strategy also in other phases of the M&A process.

3. Disruptive Automation of Growth Strategy Tasks

Dr. Karl Michael Popp

The phase M&A strategy definition is the first phase of the process model defined in [Popp,20] and describes the steps for a company to create and prepare the execution of an M&A strategy, further details in [Popp,23]. The Due Diligence phase is described in detail in [Popp,20]. Much of this section is taken from [Popp,23].

Tasks and their actions are the framework to mark up which parts of the M&A strategy phase can be automated by tools.

3.1 Overview of tasks within Growth Strategy

The following tasks make up the M&A Strategy phase:

❏ M&A Strategy.

❏ Target Screening.

❏ Simulation and modeling

Each task has a description, goals and objectives as well as data objects they are operating on. Tasks can be divided into several actions, which are also listed.

The disruptive automation of these tasks is described later in short automation scenarios.

3.2 Task M&A Strategy

Task description

The M&A strategy encompasses a holistic view, aiming to identify specific sectors and markets in which the company should proactively engage. Furthermore, it outlines the appropriate course of action for the organization within these designated areas. The M&A strategy is defined, deriving its foundation from, and complementing the overarching corporate strategy. This strategy encompasses a comprehensive and integrated approach that considers various strategic capabilities, including the current portfolio of products, services, and business models, as well as the organization's capacity to achieve success within a given market. Moreover, it considers the intellectual property (IP) strategy and the ecosystem strategy, which encompasses relationships with customers, partners, suppliers, licensors, and competitors.

When developing the M&A strategy, careful consideration is given to the existing portfolio of products, services, and business models. This ensures that any potential mergers or acquisitions align with the company's overall objectives and strengths, thus enhancing its market position and competitive advantage. Additionally, the strategy acknowledges the importance of IP and the role it plays in safeguarding the organization's innovations, patents, and copyrights.

Furthermore, the ecosystem strategy is a vital aspect of the M&A strategy, as it recognizes the significance of fostering strong relationships with key stakeholders such as customers, partners, suppliers, licensors, and even competitors. By cultivating collaborative and mutually beneficial alliances, the company can leverage synergies and create an environment conducive to innovation, growth, and long-term success.

Through the implementation of the M&A strategy, the company seeks to identify and capitalize on strategic opportunities that align with its goals and objectives.

Attributes of the Task

The task is a decision task.

The task problem is unstructured. The procedure is unclear.

The task has the following goal(s):

❑ Buyer M&A Strategy: planned

The task has the following objectives:

❑ Information asymmetry: minimized
❑ Quality: maximized
❑ Risk: minimized

❏ Synergy: maximized

The task consists of the following actions

❏ Analyze the existing strategy and identify strengths and weaknesses is automated by 3 tool(s).

❏ Analyze the existing portfolio of business models is automated by 3 tool(s).

❏ Analyse future business models is automated by 3 tool(s).

❏ Analyse future strategy is automated by 3 tool(s).

❏ Identify the strategy changes and fields of action to act upon is automated by 4 tool(s).

❏ Create an action plan how to adress strategic fields of action is automated by 2 tool(s).

❏ Define requirements for whitespaces for acquisition is automated by 3 tool(s).

The task works on the following data object types, among others:

Buyer business, Buyer strategy, Buyer M&A Strategy, Strategy, Buyer ecosystem strategy, Strategic measure of the buyer company, Assignment of strategic measures and goals of the buyer company, Strategic risks of the buyer company, Strategic assumptions of the buyer, Strategic goal of the buyer company, Hierarchy of the strategic goals of the buyer company, Buyer coverage of supply chain, Ecosystem of the buyer, Customer of the buyer, Customer segment of the buyer, Customer relationship of the buyer, Competitor of the buyer, Substitute for products of the buyer, Key partners of the buyer, Key resources of the buyer, Key activities of the buyer, Buyer's revenue streams.

Automatability

This task is partially automatable.

Tools are available.

3.3 Task Target Screening

Task description

With the result from the previous task, you have defined a space to search in and you have put requirements in place that the potential target should fulfill. First, finding targets requires a selection of the right sources to search for targets. You can look for acquisition targets in the company ecosystem, e.g. partners, suppliers, customers, competitors and in adjacent or remote markets. You can use service providers and company search databases to find appropriate targets. The search process might be iterative, so you might start with searching targets that fulfill only a few attributes, like e.g. strategy fit, size/revenue, target market fit. If you end up with a large amount of companies, you start the second iteration trying to fulfill additional attributes like business model fit, business scalability, technology fit or other attributes. Objectives of the task steer your work. You try to minimize information asymmetry by using several sources. In addition, you try to maximize the complementarity between buyer and target.

Due to incomplete information, it cannot be guaranteed that all existing, suitable targets are known to the purchasing company. For this reason, a basic set is created with the help of various sources of information, such as databases, industry experts and information on start-ups. When targets have been found, this is followed by detailed walkthrough of target candidates and a decision according to various criteria such as target competencies, region/location, sales, company size and technology attractiveness, which candidates make it onto the longlist of potential targets. From this set, companies are selected for the long list.

Attributes of the Task

The task is a decision task.

The task problem is unstructured. The task object is unstructured. The procedure is unclear.

The task has the following goal(s):

☐ Longlist of targets: created

The task has the following objectives:

☐ Information asymmetry: minimized

☐ Buyer-target complementarity: maximized

The task consists of the following actions

☐ Define selection criteria and market is automated by 6 tool(s).

☐ Scan sources for potential targets is automated by 5 tool(s).

☐ Review companies to join the longlist is automated by 5 tool(s).

☐ Define the longlist of targets is automated by 4 tool(s).

The task works on the following data object types, among others:

Target, Buyer, Target countries, Assignment of target markets to industry, Buyer Industry, Market of the target, Market of the buyer, Target company, Target locations, Longlist of targets, Ecosystem, Ecosystem of the buyer, Product of the target, Product of the buyer, Sales of the target, Target employees, Target business model, Buyer business model, Target business, Buyer business, Analyst company, Buy Side Advisor, Sell-side advisor, Market, Market Drivers, Customer of the buyer, Customer of the target, Supplier of the buyer, Supplier of the target, Cost Complementarity, Product complementarity, Brand complementarity, Target ecosystem strategy complementarity, Business model complementarity, Patent of the target, Patent, Patent of the buyer, Patent portfolio complementarity, Complementarity of countries, Financial complementarity, Complementarity of resource models, Service of the buyer, Service of the target, Services complementarity.

Automatability

This task is partially automatable.

Tools are available.

3.4   Task Simulation and modeling

Task description

The synergies from the Synergy Plan are mapped and simulated top-down to the NewCo structures and processes. It checks whether the synergies in this simulation model occur and are sustainable. In the software industry, product and cost and sales synergies are analyzed.

Attributes of the Task

The task is a decision task.

The task problem is unstructured. The task object is unstructured.

The task has the following goal(s):

☐ Synergy: analyzed

☐ Synergy plan: analyzed

The task has the following objectives:

☐ Synergy: maximized

The task works on the following data object types, among others:

Synergy, Synergy plan, Business model synergy, Synergy in the operations model, Brand complementarity, Previous acquisitions of the buyer, Complementarity of the GTM model, Complementarity of the strategy, Buyer-target complementarity, Supply chain complementarity, Market Complementarity, Complementarity of countries, Product complementarity, Cost Complementarity, Brand Synergy, Resource model synergy, GTM synergy, Strategic synergy, Market synergy, Product synergy, Cost synergy, Supply Chain Synergy, Country Synergy

Automatability

This task is partially automatable.

Equipped with this knowledge about the M&A strategy tasks we can focus now on the automation of the respective tasks.

4. ABRAMS world trade wiki for Target Screening

Dr. Jürgen Abrams

inigma LLC. ABRAMS world trade wiki is a division of inigma LLC

Target screening is one of the first tasks in the M&A process and aims to identify potential acquisition targets. The goal is to find companies that strategically, operationally, and financially fit the buyer's organization. This section highlights the basics and the importance of target screening and how ABRAMS world trade wiki automates important tasks.

4.1 Why ABRAMS world trade wiki?

The process of establishing strategic objectives is fundamentally crucial for the effective identification and subsequent selection of acquisition targets that align with the overarching goals of the organization, thereby ensuring that these targets not only fit within the desired business framework but also contribute to long-term success and sustainability.

In this context, it is imperative to discuss the key evaluation criteria that are utilized to assess potential acquisition targets, which encompass various dimensions such as market coverage, the competitive strength of the entities being evaluated, and the performance metrics associated with supply chains, all of which play a pivotal role in determining the feasibility and potential success of such acquisitions.

Furthermore, it is essential to highlight the myriad challenges that can arise during this process, including but not limited to the prevalent issue of information asymmetry, which complicates the decision-making process, alongside the necessity of establishing appropriate and well-defined selection criteria that can effectively guide the acquisition strategy.

ABRAMS world trade wiki is a powerful, sophisticated tool designed to significantly enhance transparency in the acquisition process, analyze complex supplier and customer networks with greater efficacy, and ultimately mitigate various risks that may jeopardize the success of strategic business acquisitions and partnerships.

4.2 Objectives and Strategic Alignment

Successful target screening starts with clearly defined goals, such as expanding into new geographic markets, diversifying product portfolios, or acquiring innovative technologies that complement the company's core competencies. This section describes the strategic goals for the acquisition, such as market expansion, diversification, or access to new technologies. It outlines how companies can formulate a strategic alignment.

4.3 Identifying Potential Targets

Identifying potential acquisition targets is a multi-faceted process that requires a thorough understanding of the market and specific criteria to guide the search. Companies often rely on industry analysis, competitor monitoring, and external advisors to compile a shortlist of potential targets. Key criteria for identifying potential targets include:

- ❏ Market Coverage: Assessing the target's geographic and customer market reach is essential to determine its ability to support the acquirer's strategic goals. For example, does the target operate in regions where the acquirer seeks to expand to? How well does the target's customer base align with the acquirer's growth plans? Analyzing market coverage helps identify overlaps and opportunities for new market entry.

- ❏ Competitive Strength: Evaluating the target's position within its industry involves analyzing its market share, brand reputation, and innovation capabilities. For instance, a target with a strong competitive position may contribute valuable intellectual property, advanced technology, or well-established customer relationships that can enhance the acquirer's competitive edge.

❐ Current Supply Performance: Reviewing the target's supply chain efficiency, reliability, and ability to meet demand provides insights into operational strengths and potential risks. This includes examining the target's dependency on key suppliers, its ability to adapt to supply chain disruptions, and the overall robustness of its logistics and operations. A reliable supply performance ensures that the target can sustain its operations and contribute positively to the acquirer's supply chain.

These criteria help prioritize targets that meet immediate strategic needs but also offer long-term growth potential. Approaches such as bottom-up analysis focuses on specific financial and operational data, and top-down analysis focuses on broader industry trends and strategic alignment. This ensures that selected targets align closely with the acquirer's overarching objectives and offer measurable value post-acquisition. Approaches such as bottom-up and top-down analyses further refine the search.

4.4 Evaluation Methods for Targets

Evaluating potential targets is crucial for prioritization, requiring a blend of qualitative methods, such as SWOT analyses to assess strategic fit, and quantitative methods, like financial metrics to evaluate profitability and market potential. This section presents qualitative and quantitative evaluation methods, including SWOT analyses, financial metrics, and market potential.

Leveraging Data Sources and Technologies in Screening

Modern technologies such as artificial intelligence and data analytics can significantly enhance the screening process. For example, platforms like DealCloud or PitchBook provide advanced data analytics and visualization tools to streamline the identification and evaluation of potential targets. This section explores relevant tools and platforms as well as their pros and cons.

Challenges and Best Practices

Target screening often presents a series of challenges that can impede the identification of suitable acquisition targets. One of the primary issues is information asymmetry, where critical data about potential targets is either incomplete or unavailable to the buyer. Companies frequently depend on publicly available data, which might not provide a comprehensive view of the target's financial health, operations, or strategic goals. To address this, organizations should leverage specialized databases and industry reports while engaging third-party advisors or consultants to gain deeper insights and to mitigate data gaps.

Another significant challenge is setting screening criteria that are either too broad or overly restrictive. Unrealistic criteria can lead to viable targets being overlooked or unsuitable ones being included in the selection process. Companies must ensure that their strategic priorities are clearly defined and regularly refine their criteria as new insights emerge during the screening process. This adaptability allows them to align their efforts with evolving market conditions and organizational goals.

Market dynamics and competitive pressure further complicate target screening. Rapid shifts in industry trends or intense competition can affect the availability and attractiveness of potential targets. Continuous monitoring of market trends and the development of contingency plans are essential to staying ahead of these changes. Such proactive measures enable companies to adapt their screening parameters and remain competitive in their search for suitable targets.

Finally, decision-making during target screening is often influenced by biases. For instance, organizations may overvalue well-known brands or underestimate the potential of smaller, less prominent companies. Implementing data-driven evaluation tools can help minimize subjectivity, while ensuring a diverse screening team can provide multiple perspectives and challenge preconceived notions.

By addressing these challenges and adopting best practices—such as leveraging advanced analytics tools, fostering cross-functional collaboration, and maintaining open communication with stakeholders—companies can enhance the effectiveness of their target screening process. These strategies ensure that the selected targets align with the acquirer's strategic and operational objectives, paving the way for a successful M&A transaction.

4.5 ABRAMS world trade wiki supports Target Screening

The platform ABRAMS world trade wiki, particularly its solutions for company transparency, provides significant support for the Target Screening process. By offering detailed insights into global company operations, the platform helps address key challenges:

❑ **Enhanced Information Access:** ABRAMS world trade wiki consolidates extensive data on real company activities based on customs and logistics information and can present existing supply chain relationships. This significantly reduces issues related to information asymmetry by providing detailed operational footprints. These insights enable acquirers to gain a more comprehensive understanding of potential targets and make informed decisions.

❑ **Supplier and Customer Analysis:** ABRAMS world trade wiki allows users to delve deeply into the supply chain and customer networks of potential targets. By identifying direct suppliers (Tier 1) and their suppliers (multi-tier levels), companies can assess the resilience and vulnerabilities within the target's supply chain. Similarly, analyzing direct customers and the broader customer ecosystem enables the identification of revenue stability and potential dependencies. This dual analysis is invaluable for evaluating both operational reliability and market reach.

❑ **Risk Mitigation:** Transparency into compliance records, operational dependencies, and geographic distribution helps users assess and mitigate risks. For instance, the platform highlights areas prone to geopolitical instability or environmental risks, as well as potential regulatory issues. This level of insight allows companies to proactively address vulnerabilities and safeguard their investment strategies.

❐ **Strategic Alignment:** With access to an extensive and searchable database, the platform supports the identification of companies that align with the acquirer's strategic objectives. Whether the goal is to expand geographic presence, acquire innovative technology, or strengthen market position, ABRAMS world trade wiki simplifies the process of finding targets with compatible operational and strategic characteristics.

By integrating ABRAMS world trade wiki into the screening workflow, companies enhance their ability to identify, evaluate, and prioritize potential acquisition targets. This data-driven approach improves the precision and success rate of M&A activities while reducing uncertainties in the decision-making process.

4.6 M&A Scenarios and Strategic Goals – Use-Case Selling vs. Sourcing

In the field of M&A, different strategic approaches are pursued depending on the business objectives. The following scenarios illustrate M&A strategies formed on sales or procurement, including the relevant selection criteria and key attractiveness factors of potential target companies.

In the following picture you see the different scenarios and their outputs regarding attractiveness of the target company.

M&A Target-Finder

Selling: search for an attractive M&A-Target-Company with the focus on sold products

Scenario	Strategic M&A-Goal	Currently owned company	Product and/or Country Filter	Attractiveness of Target Company
S1	Increased Salespower	Supplier A	Filtercriteria: HS-Code and/or Country	Target Company (Supplier B) with a **high** number of identical customers
S2	Increased Marketshare	Supplier A	Filtercriteria: HS-Code and/or Country	Target Company (Supplier B) with a **low** number of identical customers

Sourcing: search for an attractive M&A-Target-Company with the focus on purchased products

Scenario	Strategic M&A-Goal	Currently owned company	Product and/or Country Filter	Attractiveness of Target Company
P1	Increased Purchasingpower	Customer A	Filtercriteria: HS-Code and/or Country	Target Company (Customer B) with a **high** number of identical suppliers
P2	Increased Marketshare	Customer A	Filtercriteria: HS-Code and/or Country	Target Company (Customer B) with a **low** number of identical suppliers

Figure 4:Scenarios in M&A Target Finder

Sales-Oriented M&A Strategies ("Selling")

This strategy focuses on identifying attractive M&A targets that can enhance a company's sales performance. The attractiveness of a target company is particularly defined by whether it has a **high or low number of identical customers** to the acquiring company.

Selling Scenario S1: Increasing Sales Power

❑ Currently Owned Company: Supplier A

❑ Product/Country Filter: Selection criteria based on HS code (Harmonized System code for product classification) and/or geographical regions to target the most relevant market segments.

❑ Attractive Target: A target company (Supplier B) with a high number of identical customers.

❑ Explanation: Acquiring a supplier with a high number of shared customers creates immediate cross-selling and bundling opportunities. The combined entity can offer a broader product portfolio to the same customer base, increase wallet share, and strengthen customer relationships. Additionally, by consolidating sales forces and marketing efforts, Supplier A can improve efficiency and gain better negotiation power with key customers.

Selling Scenario S2: Increasing Market Share

❑ Currently Owned Company: Supplier A

☐ Product/Country Filter: HS code and/or geographical filters to focus on relevant market segments.

☐ Attractive Target: A target company (Supplier B) with a low number of identical customers.

☐ Explanation: This strategy is ideal for expanding into new customer segments. Since there is little overlap in the customer base, the acquisition enables Supplier A to quickly reach new markets, acquire fresh revenue streams, and diversify its risk. The integration process may require stronger efforts in aligning sales strategies, but it ultimately leads to business expansion and increased market reach.

Procurement-Oriented M&A Strategies ("Sourcing")

This approach aims to strengthen a company's purchasing power by identifying M&A targets that provide strategic advantages in procurement, supplier relations, and cost efficiencies. The attractiveness of a target company is determined by whether it has a **high or low number of identical suppliers**.

Procurement Scenario P1: Increasing Purchasing Power

☐ Currently Owned Company: Customer A

☐ Product/Country Filter: Selection based on HS code and/or geographical regions to ensure a relevant supplier network.

☐ Attractive Target: A target company (Customer B) with a high number of identical suppliers.

☐ Explanation: Acquiring a company that shares many of the same suppliers allows for volume bundling and stronger negotiation power. By combining procurement volumes, the new entity can achieve cost reductions, secure better contractual terms, and improve supply chain reliability. This strategy is particularly effective for companies looking to enhance procurement efficiency and consolidate supplier relationships.

Procurement Scenario P2: Increasing Market Share through Procurement

❏ Currently Owned Company: Customer A

❏ Product/Country Filter: Selection based on HS code and/or geographical regions.

❏ Attractive Target: A target company (Customer B) with a low number of identical suppliers.

❏ Explanation: This strategy is particularly useful for expanding the supplier network and reducing dependency on existing suppliers. By acquiring a company with a distinct supplier base, Customer A can increase supply chain flexibility, improve resilience to supplier risks, and potentially gain access to new materials, better pricing structures, or innovative production methods. Additionally, the diversification of suppliers may help mitigate risks related to geopolitical issues or supply chain disruptions.

4.7 Conclusion

Each M&A scenario is designed to optimize either the sales or procurement position of a company. The key factor in evaluating a target's attractiveness is the **degree of customer or supplier overlap**:

❏ A high number of identical customers/suppliers supports synergies, consolidation, and improved efficiency.

❏ A low number of identical customers/suppliers enables business expansion, diversification, and new market penetration.

Strategic M&A decisions require a **thorough analysis** of market structures, industry trends, and potential synergies to maximize the value generated from the transaction. ABRAMS world trade wiki provides an innovative approach tapping opaque data to deeply analyze existing supply chain relationships.

5. PATEV Value & Risk Discovery: How can IP reveal hidden values and risks in the M&A-Process

Dr.-Ing. Edelbert Häfele, Dr.-Ing. Klaus Illgner-Fehns, Dr.-Ing. Judit Inacsovszky

PATEV Associates GmbH

5.1 Customer Journey: Is IP relevant on SellSide and BuySide projects?

The M&A process is a long journey with many ups and downs. EY – one of our business partners - has put that demanding process in a nice picture with activities like climbing into mountains and crossing rivers - "a state of the art and fun to work with methodology".

In general, four phases follow each other.

M&A Strategy: Your company has a clear strategy to sell (parts of) a company and/or to buy a third-party company (or one of its business units). Key financials are in place and allow the development of an M&A profile, including a clear expectation of key markets, including related patented technologies and brand protection. AI-powered IP-based TargetSearch presents the best technology targets from around the world. Potential buyers - often larger companies with a strong IP-based market position. Potential sellers - often hidden MidCap or SME companies with a strong IP position that is being merged for value and not yet fully translated into market success.

Business Case Definition: Whenever strategy meets reality the big matching starts.

The business case now considers a specific setting. Two merging companies enter jointly in a competitive market. The business case scenario is driven by independent third-party data. Business case scenarios are the precursor of company valuation by example according to IDW S1 standard.

The business case should also be made for new market applications based on an improved patent position. Profit is king, so achieving a price premium through patent-protected technologies using well-known brands is an absolute must.

Figure 5: EY Strategy&Transaction GmbH, Dr. Georg Beckmann: B&I Journey

Due Diligence: With an attractive business case on the table, the due diligence phase can begin. All relevant assumptions need to be checked to avoid investing in risks: Overpaying or underbidding. All too often, both still happen.

Technological leadership is protected by strong patents - is this a hard fact or just a soft argument? Is the enterprise value in reasonable proportion to the independent IP value according to international standards such as IDW S5?

Post Merger Integration: This phase following signing and closing is the most challenging and integration is a must to realize the synergies. Integration is a team effort between the buy side and the sell side. The more know-how drives the combined business, the more the key development leaders/IP inventors need to be involved in the first steps of integration.

Joint IP bridges technology gaps to create a pole position for business development with new market applications through synergies based on IP-protected and highly profitable products and services.

5.2 Valuable part of the deal – which IP Assets are offered or needed?

Let's look at Intellectual Property. What are the main types of Intellectual Property and what are their main characteristics?

	Patents	Utility Models	Trademarks	Designs	Know-how / Technology
Protection	• Technical inventions	• Technical inventions (except processes)	• Brands for goods and services	• Two- or three-dimensional appearance of a product	• All available knowledge for product / service generation
Requirements	• Novelty • Inventive step: not obvious to someone skilled in that technical field • Industrially applicable	• Novelty • Inventive step: not obvious to someone skilled in that technical field • Industrially applicable	• Word, Figurative, etc. • Not descriptive or generic or contrary to public policy or morality • Distinctive characteristic	• Novelty • Individual character	• Ability of transferring the technology to a third party • Confidential
Term of protection	• Maximum 20 years	• Maximum 10 years	• Unlimited (extension every 10 years)	• Maximum 25 years	• Unlimited

Figure 6: IP summary

We use the term Intellectual Property Rights (IPR) synonymously with patents, patent applications, utility models, trademarks and designs. We use the term Know-how in a broad sense, including all intangible property such as licensed technology or confidential information, excluding patents. Know-how includes trade secrets.

Patents are granted for inventions in all fields of technology, if they are new, useful and non-obvious in the light of the "prior art" - i.e. all publicly available knowledge prior to the filing of the patent application. A patent is a set of exclusive rights, i.e. it allows its holder to prevent third parties from making, using, selling, offering for sale or importing the patented invention, except for certain forms or private and non-commercial use.

A patent application is usually published 18 months after filing. The whole examination and grant process takes several years, and in the end about 50% of applications are granted patents, often with amendments to the application, the rest being abandoned. A patent document with a separate publication number in a patent database may be a published patent application or an issued patent.

Please note that the legal function described above represents only one aspect of the broader picture! Other aspects are:

☐ Patent documents contain comprehensive descriptions of inventions, including how they are constructed, used, and their benefits compared to existing technologies.[1] This provides deep insights into a company's design and innovation processes.

☐ Patents often reveal technical details of research long before products reach the market, making them a valuable source for tracking the latest developments in a particular field.

☐ By using patent information, consulting firms and analysts can gain valuable insights into companies' financial investments, in their technological strengths and innovation strategies.

☐ The following table, compiled by PATEV and included in our IP Valuation reports, summarizes the commercial patent functions used in business contexts:

Patent function	Explanation and examples of potential effects
Protection	Premium prices due to exclusive production and / or sale; cost reduction through internal implementation
Stock / Improvement	Preventive protection of future products and processes
Obstacles to competition	Patents not used by the proprietor; additional R&D expenses for competitors being restricted who need to invent around
Cooperation currency	Access to third-party technologies, markets and property rights of third parties; compensation for current or future license agreements

---

[1] European Patent Office, "First time here? Patent information explained" [Online]. Available: https://www.epo.org/en/searching-for-patents/helpful-resources/first-time-here (accessed Jan. 30, 2025).

Patent function	Explanation and examples of potential effects
Licensing	Revenue from current or future license agreements
Transfer/sale	Revenue generation through sale
Misleading information	Misleading information about the company's development activities, intimidation of competitors
Reputation/ Motivation	Employee motivation; remuneration-based incentives; improved corporate image; improved fundraising situation

Figure 7: Patent functions

Apart from its function as a source of information, which is particularly prevalent in patents (and utility models), the most important function of IP from an M&A perspective is its potential economic value. Depending on the business context, any type of IP can be considered as an asset.

Recent observations show that intangible assets, particularly intellectual property (IP), have become an increasingly valuable component of a company's value:

❏ S&P 500 companies: intangible assets account for up to 90% of total market value in 2020 (in 1975: 17%). [2]

❏ Value chain contribution: IP and other intangibles contribute twice as much value as tangible capital to manufactured and traded products. [3]

---

[2] Ocean Tomo, "Intangible Asset Market Value Study" [Online]. Available: https://oceantomo.com/intangible-asset-market-value-study/ (accessed March 5, 2025).

[3] World Intellectual Property Organization, "Intangible Assets and Intellectual Property,", WIPO. [Online]. Available: https://www.wipo.int/en/web/intangible-assets (accessed March 5, 2025).

5.3   AI based Tools and Customized Services

In the M&A process we distinguish three phases, where different PATEV Tools, ready to use and different customized PATEV Services are applied in order to finalize a valuable deal.

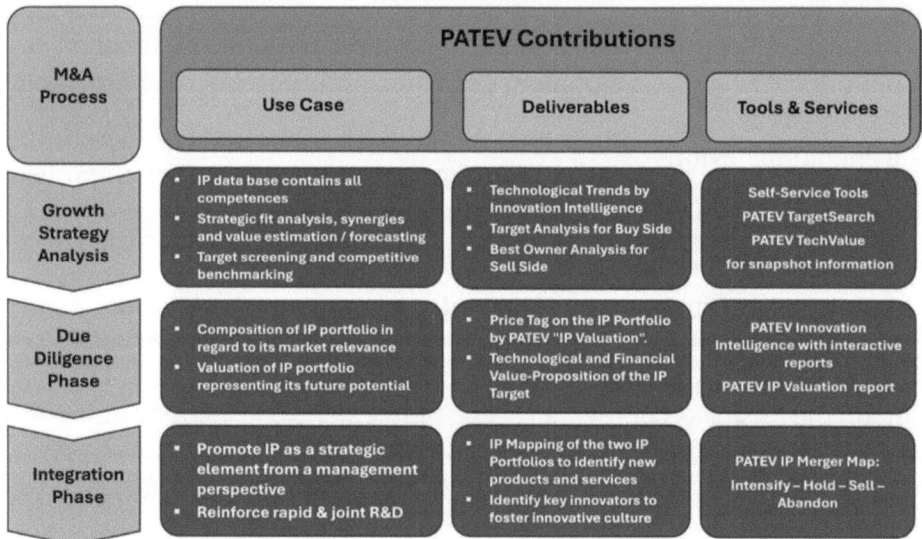

Figure 8: PATEV Contributions

5.4 Growth Strategy Analysis: Two precious minutes to find the right targets and to determine their technological leadership position

Figure 9: EY Strategy&Transaction GmbH, Dr. Georg Beckmann: B&I Journey, part 1

In this phase of the M&A Process it is most important to do a fast and reliable analysis of the names of the best targets (buy- or sell-side) and to get an instant overview of their IP based, technological leadership in the most relevant countries like EU, US, CN, JP and KR.

In sellside projects it is important to analyse instantly the relevant Corporates and their huge and international IP portfolio with thousands of Patents in ten or more languages.

In buyside project MidCap or even SME companies might be interesting. Then the analysis must be very precise in order to find also smaller corporates down to single inventors.

PATEV has developed two self-service tools against the background of patents as a source of business information and patents as a potential source of economic value.

In this context, self-service means that the tools are made available on the PATEV website and can be used by clients without the permanent assistance of PATEV. Introduction and support are part of the offer of PATEV, however.

Self Service Tool *PATEV TargetSearch*

The starting point is to characterize the topics, technologies or product areas of your interest. Your task could be to find or to evaluate companies. This should be described using a few meaningful terms. Let us show an example.

Your first input might be "automatic parking".

The tool will suggest some technology areas identified for automatic parking that may be of interest to you. You can select the most appropriate technology area descriptions for your task. The selected technology areas may contain thousands of patent documents. This is a thematic assignment by AI, not a formal one by the words.

In "expert mode" the search is narrowed and focused by some keywords ("Related Terms") of your choice (see figure below). These terms are searched in the patent text, in the next step.

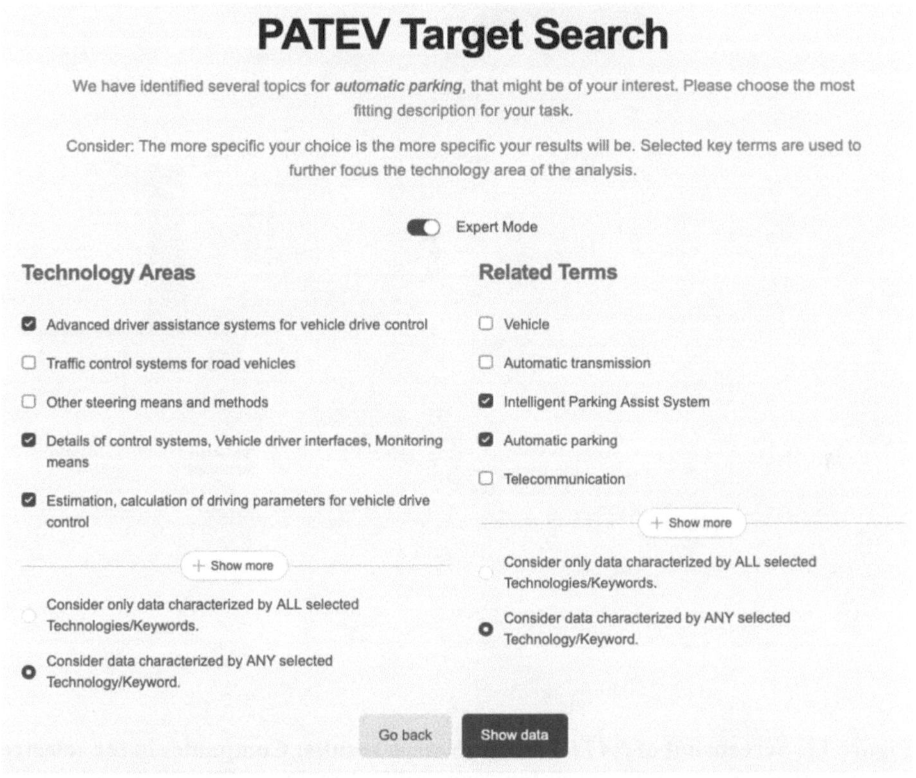

PATEV Target Search

We have identified several topics for *automatic parking*, that might be of your interest. Please choose the most fitting description for your task.

Consider: The more specific your choice is the more specific your results will be. Selected key terms are used to further focus the technology area of the analysis.

〇D Expert Mode

Technology Areas

- ☑ Advanced driver assistance systems for vehicle drive control
- ☐ Traffic control systems for road vehicles
- ☐ Other steering means and methods
- ☑ Details of control systems, Vehicle driver interfaces, Monitoring means
- ☑ Estimation, calculation of driving parameters for vehicle drive control

── + Show more ──

Consider only data characterized by ALL selected Technologies/Keywords.

○ Consider data characterized by ANY selected Technology/Keyword.

Related Terms

- ☐ Vehicle
- ☐ Automatic transmission
- ☑ Intelligent Parking Assist System
- ☑ Automatic parking
- ☐ Telecommunication

── + Show more ──

Consider only data characterized by ALL selected Technologies/Keywords.

○ Consider data characterized by ANY selected Technology/Keyword.

Go back   Show data

Figure 10: Screenshot *PATEV TargetSearch* Technology Area and Related Terms selection

On the next screen you can move the mouse over the map to see the companies with the most patent families over the last 5 years in the selected technology areas and regions of the map. You can use the Export data function to get the full list of patent applicants (companies).

The top right shows the distribution of patent applicants across Europe, North America, Japan, China and South Korea. Below are the companies with the most patent families worldwide.

A patent family comprises patents/patent applications for the same invention in different countries and regions. *PATEV TargetSearch* works internally on the basis of patent families.

The regional allocation is based on the location of the headquarters/patenting subsidiaries of the companies.

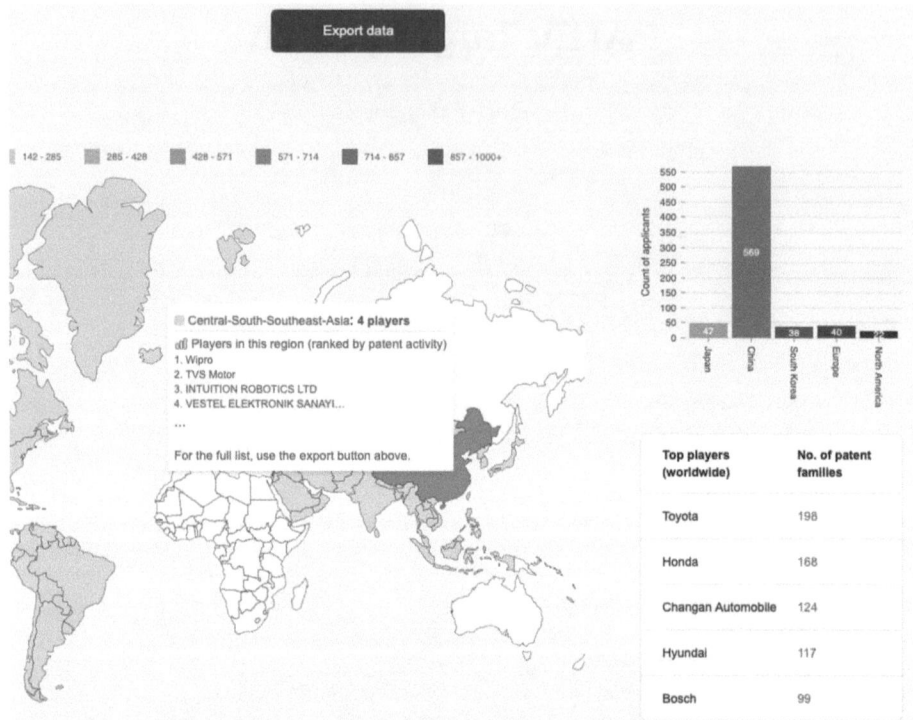

Figure 11: Screenshot of *PATEV TargetSearch* results: Companies in the selected technology areas, "mouse over" for geographical regions of the headquarters

The following M&A relevant questions can be answered with this AI-based search and analysis called *TargetSearch:*

❏ Which companies are currently dominant in your technology/product area and geographical region of interest (indicated by the number of their patent families)?

❏ Which companies are the leading developers today and the key market players of the future? (Recent patent applications indicate current development activity and new current or planned products and services.)

❏ In which geographical regions are the most recent patenting (=developing, with actual or planned production) companies located?

❏ What is the ratio of the recent patent family volumes between companies? This is an indication of recent or projected product/service sales value or market share proportions.

Self Service Tool *PATEV TechValue*

In the other self-service tool, the starting point is entering a company name. This company could, for example, be involved in an M&A scenario.

The main point of interest is to check whether the Target-company's technological position correlates with substantial economic value by leadership in EU, US, JP, CN or KR.

Your first input might be "Atriva Therapeutics". This is a fictitious example, the start-up company has no connection with any known transactions or PATEV projects.

PATEV Tech Value Intelligence

We have identified the following companies, that might be of your interest. Please choose the most fitting company name(s). Up to three selections can be included in the analysis.

Consider: The company names are based on the patent assignees given on the underlying patent documents. The more specific your choice in the list given below the more specific your results will be.

Above are the companies with the most patents!

Company selection

Select companies (up to 3)

ATRIVA THERAPEUTICS GMBH

Figure 12: Screenshot of *PATEV TechValue*: Company name selection

You select the "right" company names from a list that pops up – these are the patent applicant names that most closely match your input.

In the next step, the tool will suggest some technology areas identified on the base of the alive patents of the selected patent applicant (company or companies).

Here, "alive" or "active" means that the patents or patent applications are pending or granted and not ceased. Patents or patent applications may expire or be abandoned for a variety of reasons. For example, the products in which they were implemented are no longer manufactured.

The owner decides not to pay the patent fees to the patent office and the patent lapses. The (simplified) legal status is "dead" from that point on. A dead patent is part of the state of the art, but it has no protective or restrictive legal force, so it has no value. The maximum term of patents can be 20 years, but this is rarely achieved. This is the case, for example, with standard-essential patents in telecommunications or in the manu-facturing of pharmaceuticals.

The *PATEV TechValue* tool is based on alive patent documents with separate document numbers that are considered and counted (unlike *TargetSearch*, which considers patent families from the last 5 years).

You can select the most appropriate technology area descriptions for your task. The selected technology areas may contain thousands of pa-tent documents, it is a thematic assignment by AI, not a formal one by the words.

In "expert mode" the search is narrowed and focused by some keywords ("Related Terms") of your choice. These terms are then searched in spe-cific patent text blocks.

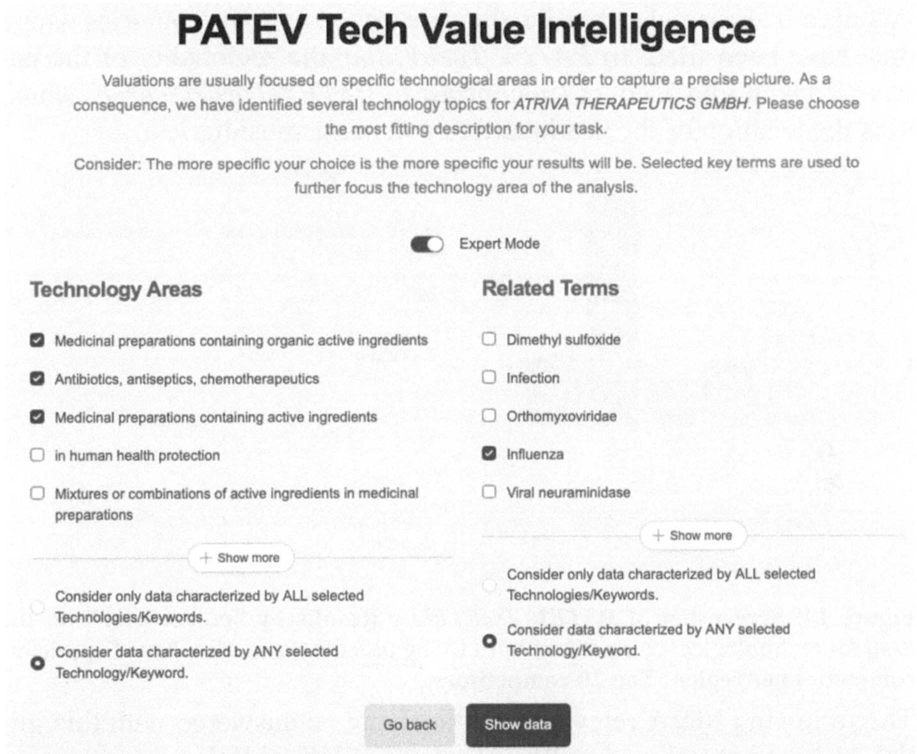

PATEV Tech Value Intelligence

Valuations are usually focused on specific technological areas in order to capture a precise picture. As a consequence, we have identified several technology topics for *ATRIVA THERAPEUTICS GMBH*. Please choose the most fitting description for your task.

Consider: The more specific your choice is the more specific your results will be. Selected key terms are used to further focus the technology area of the analysis.

Expert Mode

Technology Areas

- ☑ Medicinal preparations containing organic active ingredients
- ☑ Antibiotics, antiseptics, chemotherapeutics
- ☑ Medicinal preparations containing active ingredients
- ☐ in human health protection
- ☐ Mixtures or combinations of active ingredients in medicinal preparations

+ Show more

Consider only data characterized by ALL selected Technologies/Keywords.

○ Consider data characterized by ANY selected Technology/Keyword.

Related Terms

- ☐ Dimethyl sulfoxide
- ☐ Infection
- ☐ Orthomyxoviridae
- ☑ Influenza
- ☐ Viral neuraminidase

+ Show more

Consider only data characterized by ALL selected Technologies/Keywords.

○ Consider data characterized by ANY selected Technology/Keyword.

Go back   Show data

Figure 13: Screenshot *PATEV TechValue:* Technology Area and Related Terms selection

On the next screen, you can move the mouse over the map to see the companies with the most living patent documents in the selected technology areas and geographical regions of the map. You can use the Export data function to obtain the list of patent applicants (companies), including the selected ones, sorted by the number of living patent documents, in separate sheets for the different countries and regions. In our showcase, the selected startup company has a very good ranking in Europe and in the US as well (in the export file, not shown here).

The lower left part of the figure shows the distribution of patent applicants (companies) with the most active patents in Europe, North America, Japan, China and South Korea. The bottom right part shows the companies with the most active patents worldwide.

Patents are territorial rights, i.e. they are effective in the countries where they have been filed. In *PATEV TechValue*, the regionality of the patents is taken into account (in contrast to *PATEV TargetSearch,* which uses the location of the headquarters/patenting subsidiaries).

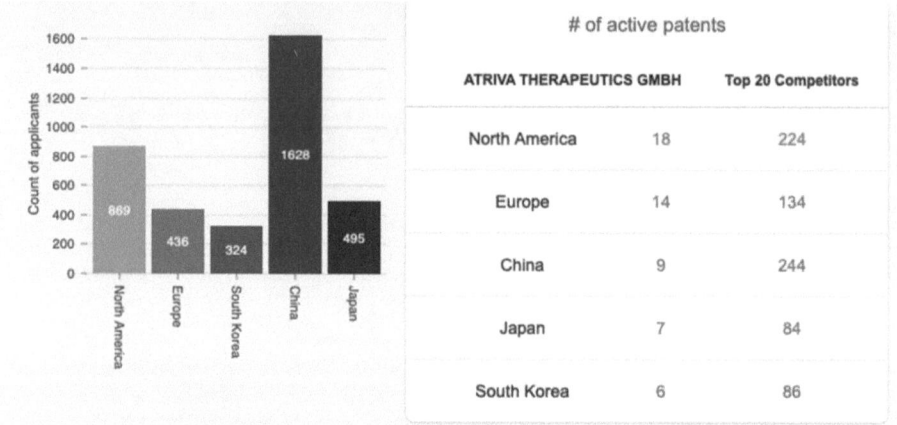

Figure 14: Screenshot of *PATEV TechValue:* Results by "mouse over" on the map for technological competitors with living patents there. Number of applicant companies per region, Top 20 competitors.

The following M&A relevant questions can be answered with this initial AI-based search and analysis tool *PATEV TechValue:*

❑ Are there any patents pending or granted with the company in your mind (your client), as applicant/owner?

❑ In which technology areas (as defined by AI) and countries are the patents of it?

❑ In which regions/countries are the most third party (competitor) patents in these Technology Areas?

❑ What is your client's patent position compared to its technological competitors? How many patents do they have compared to your client, in different countries/regions?

❑ (Technological competitors: Companies with patents or patent applications in the same technological area(s) as your client. They can be potential suppliers or customers of your client as well.)

❏ Does your client's patent portfolio have potential monetary value based on its position in the competitive environment?

Together, the two PATEV Self-Service Tools provide a very good picture of patent positioning and thus an indication of the market positioning of technology-based companies, including those with computer-implemented inventions.

6. Disruptive automation of due diligence

Dr. Karl Michael Popp

Looking at disruptive automation, let us first identify some of the key tasks during the due diligence phase, which we will cover later in automation scenarios.

6.1 Overview of tasks within the due diligence phase

The following tasks are contained in the due diligence phase:

❏ Commercial due diligence with its subtasks
- ❏ Financial Due Diligence
- ❏ Operational Due Diligence
- ❏ Due Diligence of the target's strategy
- ❏ GTM Due Diligence

❏ Valuation

❏ SPA creation

6.2 Task Commercial Due Diligence

Task description

> The target business model is analysed in detail and compared with the buyer business model. This is done in the subtasks of this task. The differences between the business models are documented and any steps that may be necessary for a potential integration are included in the draft business model integration plan. The complementarity between the business models of the buyer and the target company are also considered.

Attributes of the Task

The task is a decision task.

The task problem is structured.

The task has the following goal(s):

- ☐ Target business model: adjusted
- ☐ Draft Business Model Integration Plan: prepared

The task has the following objectives:

- ☐ Risk: minimized
- ☐ Quality: maximized
- ☐ Information asymmetry: minimized

The task has the following subtasks

- ☐ Financial Due Diligence
- ☐ Operational Due Diligence
- ☐ Due Diligence of the target's strategy
- ☐ GTM Due Diligence

The task consists of the following actions

- ☐ Check the business model

The task works on the following data object types, among others:

Key resources of the target, Key partners of the target, Ecosystem, Structure of the target costs, Channel of the target, Key activities of the target, Target value proposition, Business model difference, Buyer business model, Draft Business Model Integration Plan, Target business model, Business model synergy

Questions to be used during the execution of the task

The task is executed with the following questions, among others:

- ☐ What are the target's products and services?
- ☐ How do the target's products and services distinguish themselves from those of competitors?
- ☐ What is the target's value proposition?
- ☐ What are the target's customer segments?
- ☐ What is the problem addressed by the target, what are the customers of the individual customer segments?

- ❑ Which added value do the products and services provide to customers?
- ❑ Can it be assumed that the target's products and services will continue to be in demand by customers in the future?
- ❑ What are the target's business models?
- ❑ How is revenue generated?
- ❑ How crisis-proof and scalable is the revenue model?
- ❑ How is revenue distributed among the customer segments?
- ❑ Which channels does the target company use to interact with customers (segments)?
- ❑ On which digital channels does the target company interact with the customers (segments)?
- ❑ Which partners does the target company work with?
- ❑ What are the forms of partnerships with distribution partners?
- ❑ Does the target operate a platform business model?
- ❑ Which employees are indispensable for service delivery (key resources)?
- ❑ Which technical resources are indispensable for service delivery (key resources)?
- ❑ Which intellectual property is indispensable for service provision (Key Resources)?
- ❑ Which partners are indispensable for service provision (Key Resources)?
- ❑ What are the activities that are indispensable for service delivery and the value proposition of the target?
- ❑ What is the cost structure of the business model and how do costs behave as the company grows?
- ❑ Do the cost structure and revenue generation allow for a sustainable profit?
- ❑ How can the business models of target and buyer complement each other?

❑ Which synergies can result from the complementarities of the business models of target and buyer?

❑ How does the value proposition of the target fit with the buyer?

❑ How do the target customer segments fit the buyer?

❑ How do the problems addressed by the target fit the buyer?

❑ Which joint added value by solving problems will the products and services of the target and the buyer offer customers in the future?

❑ How does the way in which sales are generated suit the buyer?

❑ How do the channels of interaction of the customer and the target with the customer fit together?

❑ Can the buyer's products and services be sold through the target's channels?

❑ Are the technical resources of the target and the buyer complementary?

❑ Can the target's intellectual property be used by the buyer?

❑ Which influence does the acquisition have on the cost structure of the buyer and target?

❑ Are there complementarities between buyer and target in the partner ecosystem?

❑ Which applications are used in modeling and controlling business models?

Automatability

This task is partially automatable. There are tools for semi-automated creation and management of business models. The action "Check business model" can be automated but is not usually performed automatically.

6.3 Task Operational Due Diligence

Task description

The Operations Model implements the business models of a company by allocating resources from the resource model. The operations due diligence covers the implementation of all aspects of the business model and includes in particular the examination of all operational processes of a company, including administrative processes, sales, supply chain and production processes. Since there can be numerous operation models for a business model, it must be checked whether optimal implementation of the business model has been chosen with regard to the integration goals. In addition, the resources, capacities, process flows, and the risks associated with the operations are analyzed and activities for designing the operations integration plan are collected.

Attributes of the Task

The task is a decision task.

The task problem is structured.

The task has the following goal(s):

❏ Target operations model: analyzed

❏ Draft Operations Integration Plan: prepared

The task has the following objectives:

❏ Information asymmetry: minimized

❏ Integration success: maximized

The task has the following subtasks

❏ Production Due Diligence

❏ Sustainability and ESG Due Diligence

❏ Supplier Due Diligence

❏ Customer Due Diligence

❏ IT Due Diligence

❏ Technical Due Diligence

❏ Human Resources Due Diligence

❏ Cultural Due Diligence

The task works on the following data object types, among others:

Draft Operations Integration Plan, Product of the target, Service, Supplier of the target, Supplier relationship, Supply chain, Target business, Target company, Operations of the target GTM activities, Operations of the target production, Target coverage of supply chain, Target operations model, Synergy in the operations model, Risk of the target operations model

Questions to be used during the execution of the task

The task is executed with the following questions, among others:

- ☐ In which way is the value proposition of the target transported to the customers?
- ☐ How are the target's customer segments addressed and supported?
- ☐ How can the added value of the products and services be measured for the customer?
- ☐ How is each individual business model of the target implemented operationally?
- ☐ How is revenue planned, initiated and generated?
- ☐ How does the target company interact with its customers (segments)?
- ☐ How is the interaction on channels implemented operationally?
- ☐ Which partners does the target company work with and in what way?
- ☐ What is the value proposition for the partners?
- ☐ Which resources are indispensable for service delivery (key resources) and how are they tied to the company in the long term?
- ☐ What are the key activities that are indispensable for service delivery and the value proposition of the target?
- ☐ Can the key activities be protected against imitation?
- ☐ Do the key activities scale with the planned revenue?
- ☐ Can the planned cost structure of the business model be maintained or improved as the company grows?

❏ Do the cost structure and revenue generation allow a sustainable profit?

❏ Which applications are used to implement the operational model?

❏ What is to be done in concrete terms to achieve synergies from the complementarities between the target and buyer operation models?

Automatability

This task is partially automatable. Individual actions can be partially automated. Details can be found in the individual subtasks.

6.4   Task Supplier Due Diligence

Task description

All target suppliers and supplier relationships are being analyzed and reviewed.Risk is being evaluated for each of the supplier relationships.

Attributes of the Task

The task is a decision task.

The task problem is structured.

The task has the following goal(s):

❏   Supplier of the target: analyzed

The task has the following objectives:

❏ Information asymmetry: minimized

❏ Integration success: maximized

The task consists of the following actions

❏   Assess supplier relationships is automated by 2 tool(s).

❏   Assess supplier performance is not automated.

❏   Assess supply chain complementarity is automated by 3 tool(s).

❏   Assess supply chain risk is automated by 2 tool(s).

The task works on the following data object types, among others:

Supplier of the target, Vendor contract, Supplier relationship, Supply chain, Material supplier of the target company, Service supplier of the target, Production material of the target company, Target coverage of supply chain, Supply chain complementarity, Supply Chain Synergy,

Automatability

This task is partially automatable.

6.5　Task Sustainability and ESG Due Diligence

Task description

This task evaluates environmental impact and environmental compliance of a target company and its supply chain. The evaluation process generally encompasses a comprehensive examination of various elements such as environmental permits which govern the legal utilization of natural resources, meticulous compliance records that detail adherence to environmental laws and regulations, issues pertaining to contamination that may arise from previous industrial activities or accidental spills, practices associated with waste management that ensure the safe disposal and treatment of hazardous and non-hazardous materials, as well as potential liabilities that may emerge in relation to pollution, hazardous substances, and violations of established regulatory frameworks that are designed to protect public health and the environment.

Attributes of the Task

The task is a decision task.

The task problem is structured.

The task has the following goal(s):

☐　Environmental risk of the target: analyzed

The task has the following objectives:

☐ Information asymmetry: minimized

☐ Risk: minimized

The task consists of the following actions

☐ Check environmental permits is not automated.

☐ Check compliance with environmental compliance with laws and regulations is not automated.

☐ Check production sites for contamination is not automated.

☐ Evaluate waste management practices is not automated.

☐ Evaluate environmental aspects of the supply chain is automated by 1 tool(s).

☐ Evaluate potential liabilities reg. pollution, violation of regulations reg. health and environment is not automated.

The task works on the following data object types, among others:

Company environment, Risk of the target, Energy requirement in the production of the target, Hazardous material of the target company, Corporate environmental policies of the target, Environmental reports of the target

Questions to be used during the execution of the task

The task is executed with the following questions, among others:

☐ Are there any voluntary commitments that go beyond the legal standards, if so, have they been met?

☐ Documentation: Are the waste approval and waste information sheet for controllable waste complete?

☐ Has environmental damage or risk been identified (and if so, to what extent)?

☐ Has the company carried out consistent PR in the environmental sector?

- ❏ Have remediation or audit mandates been issued by the authorities or are administrative proceedings pending for environmental damage or risks?
- ❏ Have any environmental investigations been carried out into known or potential environmental damage?
- ❏ Have any environmental investigations ever been carried out?
- ❏ Have remediation concepts been developed with regard to such environmental damage or have any remediation measures been carried out at all?
- ❏ How were the premises of the companies used in the past?
- ❏ Waste management concept: is there a coherent waste management concept?
- ❏ What is influenced by the environmental damage or hazards identified (soil, other media (in particular groundwater, soil air, air), buildings (asbestos?)
- ❏ Which products, production processes from the past can lead to liability?

Automatability

This task is partially automatable.

6.6 Task Valuation

Task description

The valuation for the independent target is created. Assumptions and accounting selection rules of the target are taken into account. The valuation calculation can be based on comparison values (comps) or on a complete valuation calculation, e.g. on a net present value. The complete valuation is often carried out using the buyer's cost structures to achieve a suitable representation from the buyer's point of view. Values from companies in the same industry and/or of the same size are used for the evaluation using comparison values.

Attributes of the Task

The task is a decision task.

The task problem is structured.

The task has the following goal(s):

☐ Target valuation: prepared

The task has the following objectives:

☐ Information asymmetry: minimized

☐ Risk: minimized

The task consists of the following actions

☐ Calculate valuation

The task works on the following data object types, among others:

Target valuation, Sales of the target, Revenue streams of the target, Cost of the target, Structure of the target costs, Target company tax, HR costs of the target, Production costs of the target company, GTM costs of the target, Target IT Costs, Tax costs of target, Costs of third party patent licenses, Cost Complementarity, Financial complementarity, Cost of the buyer, Buyer cost structure, Profitability of the target, Accounting guidelines, Application of accounting and valuation options, Preferred convertible bond of the target, Target's liabilities, Target bank, Debts of the target, Convertible bonds

Questions to be used during the execution of the task

The task is executed with the following questions, among others:

☐ What are the target's sales with each relevant product and service and how are they treated in accounting terms?

☐ How high are the costs of the target and how are these treated for accounting purposes?

☐ What is the working capital of the target?

☐ How high are the target's liabilities and the associated debt service?

- ❏ Which environmental factors influence the target's financial performance?
- ❏ What are the costs of generating sales in different channels?
- ❏ Which accounting selection rules should be followed? Which changes to the accounting selection rules must we expect when we take over?
- ❏ Which cost rates of the buyer should be used for the valuation calculation?
- ❏ Which cash benefits, convertible bonds and stock options will Target employees receive?
- ❏ How is the pension scheme regulated?

Automatability

This task is partially automatable. Automated tools are available for the action 'Calculate evaluation', but the data usually has to be compiled and cleaned up manually.

6.7 Task Share Purchase Agreement creation

Task description

Assumptions and negotiation positions, like e.g. non-negotiables are defined. The results of the valuation calculation and the planning of the financing of the acquisition are also considered in the preparation. Then, the deal is negotiated, and appropriate contract documents are prepared. Details of the contract, such as the purchase price, further contractual terms and conditions as well as the closing conditions are negotiated on the basis of the due diligence results, the evaluation of the target, the deal financing plans and the integration plans. If preliminary negotiations took place, the results of the due diligence are used for renegotiations.

Attributes of the Task

The task is a decision task.

The task problem is structured.

The task has the following goal(s):
☐ Deal contract: negotiated

The task has the following objectives:
☐ Risk: minimized
☐ Integration success: maximized

The task consists of the following actions
☐ Planning of the negotiation is automated by 1 tool(s).
☐ Exchange and discussion of negotiation positions is automated by 1 tool(s).
☐ Agreement on contract contents is automated by 1 tool(s).
☐ Conclusion of the negotiations is automated by 1 tool(s).
☐ Re-evaluate deal risk is automated by 1 tool(s).

The task works on the following data object types, among others:

Business plan, Deal, Deal breaker, Deal proposal, Negotiating position, Negotiable position, Non-negotiable position, Deal contract, Provisions clause, Indemnifications clause, Covenants clause, Warranties clause, Representations clause, Success factor, Synergy plan, Deal Financing Concept, Taxation of the acquisition project, Integrated valuation for NewCo, Strategic assumptions of the buyer, Due Diligence results, Deal risk

Questions to be used during the execution of the task

The task is executed with the following questions, among others:
☐ What is the buyer's reservation purchase price?
☐ Which interval should the purchase price be in?
☐ How should the purchase price be paid?
☐ Should a deposit or retention of part of the purchase price be negotiated?
☐ Which are the minimum assurances and warranties that the seller should give?

❏ Which representations and warranties of the seller regarding his intellectual property should be set out in the contract?

❏ Which covenants should be included in the deal contract?

❏ Which clauses related to provisions are needed in the deal contract?

❏ Which indemnification clauses should be included in the deal contract?

❏ Which agreements between signature and conclusion should the contract contain?

❏ Which risks does the buyer wish to assume?

❏ How should the assumption of liability be regulated?

❏ What will be the time frame for signing and closing?

❏ Which contract elements should be included for successful merger integration?

❏ How will risks and problems be handled after signing or closing?

Automatability

This task is partially automatable. The action "negotiation" would be automatable but is usually not performed automatically.

Tools are available.

7. ABRAMS world trade wiki for Due Diligence

Dr. Jürgen Abrams

inigma LLC. ABRAMS world trade wiki is a division of inigma LLC

Due diligence is a vital component of the M&A process and involves a detailed review of the target. This includes analyzing financial data such as balance sheets and income statements, legal documentation including contracts and compliance records, operational metrics like supply chain efficiency, and intangible assets such as intellectual property and brand value. The goal is to identify risks and opportunities to make informed decisions. This section explains the basics and the significance of due diligence and where ABRAMS world trade wiki supports this step of an M&A process.

7.1 Why ABRAMS world trade wiki for DD?

The examination centers on a comprehensive analysis that encompasses the financial, operational, and strategic dimensions pertaining to a particular target company, thereby facilitating an in-depth understanding of its overall performance and market positioning.

The breadth of this examination encompasses a comprehensive review of both vendors and clients, a meticulous evaluation of supply chain weaknesses and threats, alongside a detailed investigation into the essential importance of performing Environmental, Social, and Governance (ESG) due diligence within the current corporate environment.

ABRAMS world trade wiki serves as a valuable resource for identifying concealed risks, conducting a meticulous analysis of supply chain intelligence, and effectively benchmarking competitive positions within the broader market framework.

7.2 Operational Due Diligence

This section focuses on evaluating the target's operational processes, products purchased or sold. Business partners and supply chain details are analyzed. A thorough operational due diligence process includes the following subcategories:

Supplier Due Diligence

Understanding the target's supplier landscape is crucial to mitigating risks and ensuring operational stability post-acquisition. Key evaluation criteria include:

- ☐ **Supply chain Risk Mitigation**: Assess the target's ability to manage risks within its supply chain. This includes analyzing exposure to critical suppliers, identifying alternate sourcing strategies, and evaluating the potential impact of geopolitical risks or natural disasters on supply continuity.
- ☐ **Check Direct Suppliers (Tier 1)**: Review the target's relationships with its immediate suppliers by examining existing contracts, delivery performance, and quality standards. This helps to determine supplier reliability and whether current agreements align with the strategic goals of the acquiring company.
- ☐ **Identify Suppliers of Suppliers (Multi-Tier Levels)**: Investigate the broader supply chain network beyond direct suppliers to identify vulnerabilities in the multi-tier structure. This involves assessing second tier and beyond suppliers for their dependency on critical raw materials or critical suppliers, which could introduce hidden risks to the target's operations.

Customer Due Diligence

Analyzing the customer base is equally critical to understanding revenue stability and market reach. Key evaluation criteria include:

- ☐ **Supply chain Risk Mitigation**: Evaluate the risks related to customer dependencies, such as reliance on a few large customers or the potential for demand fluctuations caused by market or economic changes. This analysis helps identify areas where the customer base may need diversification to reduce risk.

❑ **Check Direct Customers**: Assess the target's relationships with its primary customers by analyzing customer satisfaction metrics, revenue concentration, and the stability of existing contracts. Understanding these factors helps determine the sustainability of the target's revenue streams and potential opportunities for upselling or cross-selling.

❑ **Identify Customers of Customers (Multi-Tier Level)**: Investigate the downstream customer ecosystem to understand how the target's products or services impact end-users. By analyzing the broader demand drivers and potential bottlenecks in the multi-tier customer network, companies can identify risks and opportunities that influence long-term revenue growth and market reach.

Sustainability and ESG Due Diligence

This topic explores the assessment of environmental, social, and governance (ESG) factors and their growing importance in the M&A process. However, as Sustainability and ESG is currently not the main focus of ABRAMS world trade wiki, it will not be further described here.

7.3 ABRAMS world trade wiki – Insights during the Due Diligence

The platform ABRAMS world trade wiki offers powerful tools and resources to enhance various aspects of the due diligence process. Through its solutions for company transparency, supply chain intelligence, and competitive intelligence, the platform addresses critical challenges in the following ways:

Company Transparency

This solution provides comprehensive profiles of potential targets, including suppliers, customers, purchasing volume, sales volume as well as information on product prices. Access to such detailed information helps uncover hidden risks and ensure a thorough understanding of the target's operations and governance.

The illustrated example presents a comprehensive Sankey Diagram that meticulously delineates the principal suppliers along with the corresponding customers associated with a hypothetical target company called "Continental Autonomous Mobility".

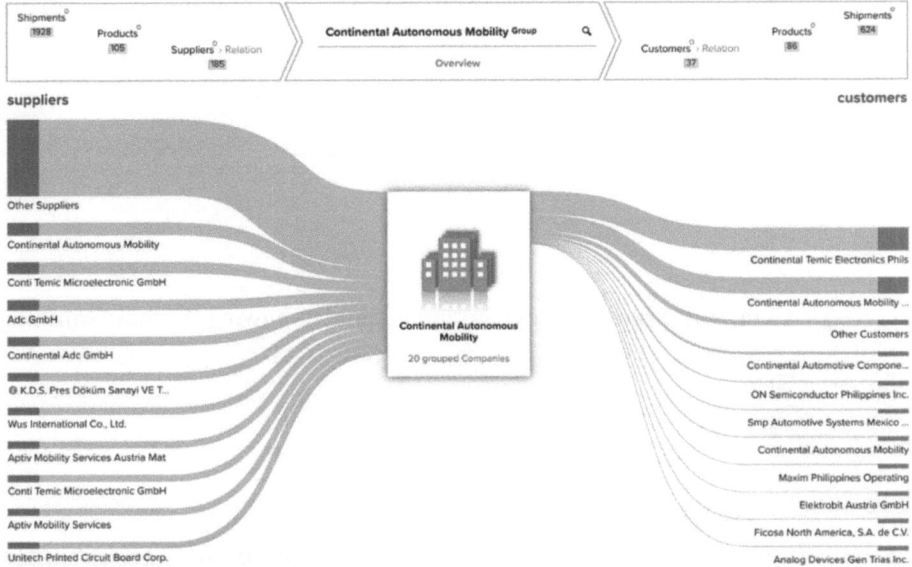

Figure 15: Company Transparency: Sankey Diagram with suppliers and customers

The following example relates to an anonymized apparel importer. The detailed shipment information in the next picture provides an exhaustive overview regarding the predominant nations from which the apparel company imports from with a significant and noteworthy emphasis placed on Bangladesh, which serves as the paramount source of the imported goods that are integral to their operational framework. Further countries are India, Pakistan, Indonesia, and Vietnam.

Shipment	Supplier	Country	Customer	Country	Notify Party	Product Description	HS Code
40,287 entries found							
1 — 2024-11-30 (shipping)	Pakiza Knit Com Ltd. A-1/5, Majidpur, Bolmeher, Sav 1340 Savar Ps,	Supplier Country — Bangladesh 22,013; India 6,506; Pakistan 3,877; Indonesia 78; Viet Nam 76; Europe (1) 2,274; Turkey 2,274	Shipments	Germany		GIRL'S DRESS	610442
2 — 2024-11-30 (shipping)	S.M Sourcing Beimal, Konaba Gazipur Sadar, Sadar Ps, Gazip Bangladesh			Germany		BABY SHORTS – 9,736 PACK	611120
3 — 2024-11-30 (shipping)	Pakiza Knit Com Ltd. A-1/5, Majidpur, Bolmeher, Sava 1340 Savar Ps,			Germany		GIRL'S DRESS	610442
4 — 2024-11-30 (shipping)	Pakiza Knit Com Ltd. A-1/5, Majidpur, Bolmeher, Savar, Dhaka 1340 Savar Ps, Dhaka-...			Germany		GIRL'S DRESS	610442
5 — 2024-11-30 (shipping)	S.M Sourcing Beimal, Konabari, Gazipur Sadar, Gazipur Sadar Ps, Gazipur-1700 Bangladesh	Bangladesh	KIk Textilien Und Non Food GmbH Sie	Germany		LADIES T-SHIRT	610910

Figure 16: Company Transparency: Shipment details showing the main sourcing countries

 Scan this QR code to view the figure online.

In the subsequent illustration, we will examine yet another anonymized import company specializing in apparel, whose main source for acquiring goods predominantly stems from the diverse and vibrant market of India. In the accompanying image, one can observe a detailed breakdown of the shipment particulars, which furnish an extensive and thorough overview of the key sourcing nations that are intricately linked with that theoretical target enterprise, providing valuable insights into its supply chain dynamics.

19,538 entries found								
Shipment	Supplier	Country	Customer	Country	Notify Party	Product Description		HS Code
1	Himanshu App Ltd.	Supplier Country ✓	Shipments	Unknown Country, Company Identified		RMG 100% VISCOSE WOVEN LADIES LONG PANTS		620463
2024-11-30 (registration)		Asia (3)	19,311					
2	Himanshu App Ltd.	India	17,894	Germany		RMG 100% COTTON WOVEN LADIES BLOUSE (OE		62063090
		Bangladesh	1,414					
2024-11-30 (registration)		Pakistan	3					
3	Himanshu App Ltd.	Europe (1)	71	Unknown Country, Company Identified		RMG 100% VISCOSE WOVEN LADIES BLOUSE WIT		62114390
		Turkey	71					
2024-11-30 (registration)		Unknown (1)	156					
4	Knit Bazaar (Pv 40-41 Vadam, T Gazipur-1711 Ba		GO	Germany		LADIES KNITTED BLOUSONS.		610220
2024-11-30 (shipping)								
5	Kay Vee Fashion No. 1, Nethaji Nagar First St, Karumarampelayam, Uthukuli Road, Tirupur / Tamil Nadu IN	India	Ernsting Family GmbH & Co. KG- Hugo-Ernsting-Platz/Industriestrasse 1 48653 Coefeld-Lette	Germany		95% COTTON 5% ELASTHANE KNITTED CHILDRE		61099090
2024-11-30 (registration)								

Figure 17: Company Transparency: Shipment details of another target showing the main sourcing countries

 Scan this QR code to view the figure online.

Supply Chain Intelligence

Supply chain intelligence allows users to analyze the supply chain network of the target, including identifying key suppliers, their locations, and dependencies. This helps in:

❏ **Risk Assessment**: Evaluating potential supply chain vulnerabilities, such as reliance on a single supplier or exposure to geopolitical risks.

❏ **Operational Insights**: Gaining clarity on supply chain efficiency and adaptability to disruptions, ensuring the target's operational stability post-acquisition.

The next screenshot provides a comprehensive overview of the potential vulnerabilities within the supply chain of „Infinera Corp", which may arise from factors such as an over-dependence on a singular supplier or the heightened exposure to various geopolitical risks that can significantly impact operations.

ABRAMS world trade wiki serves as a robust tool that facilitates the automatic identification of shipments originating from suppliers who may potentially be implicated in geopolitical risks, including but not limited to regions such as China and the Russian Federation, thus enhancing risk management strategies and decision-making processes.

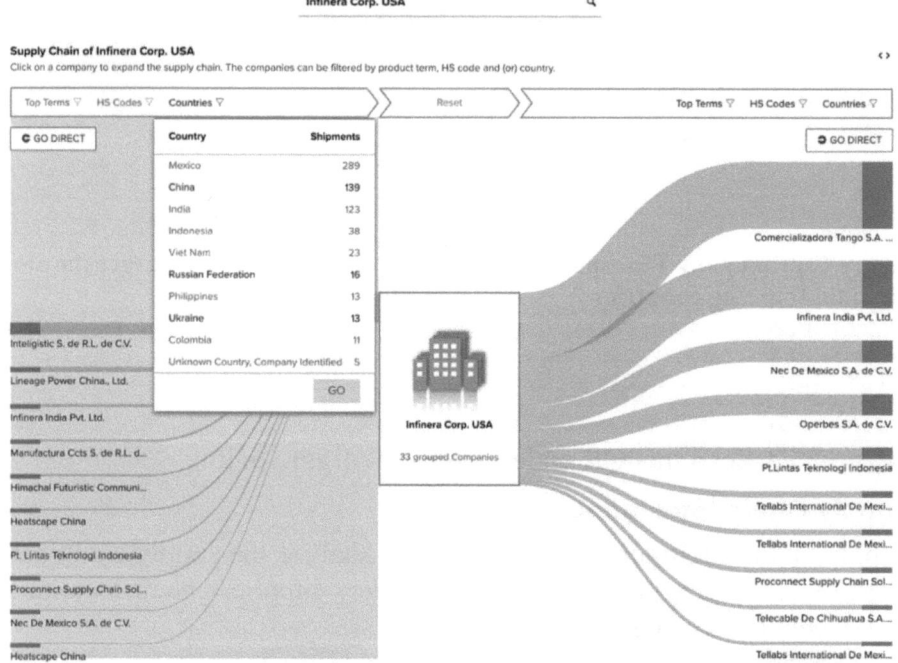

Figure 18: Supply Chain Intelligence: Automatically identifying shipments from suppliers

The following picture provides a comprehensive demonstration of the methods employed to assess possible weaknesses within the supply chain framework, extending our focus well beyond just the immediate tier one suppliers. In the realm of Supply Chain Intelligence, this involves the critical process of pinpointing and analyzing shipments originating from various suppliers that may be at risk due to geopolitical uncertainties, thereby transcending the limitations imposed by merely considering Tier 1 suppliers and embracing a Multi-Tier-Transparency approach.

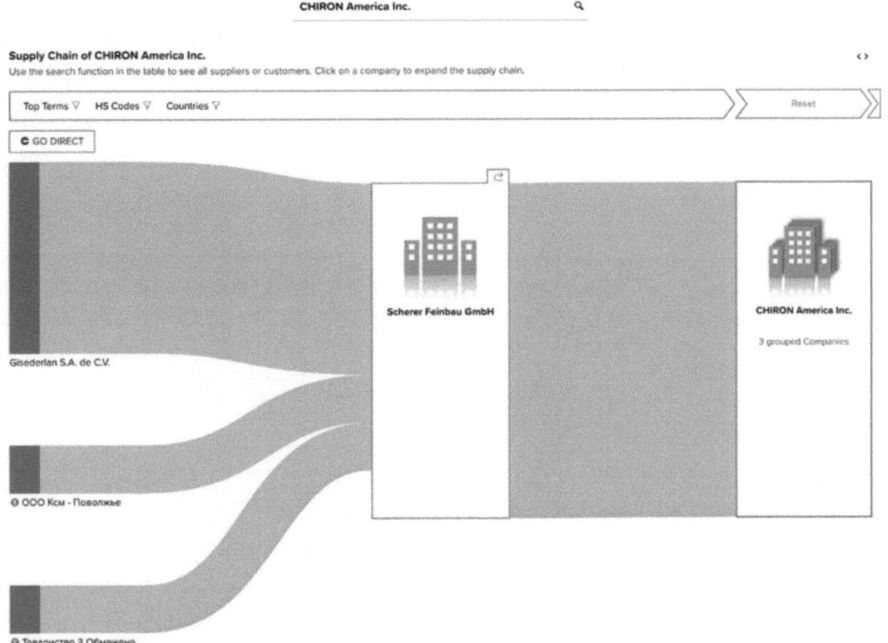

Figure 19: Supply Chain Intelligence: identifying shipments with geopolitical risks – beyond Tier 1 (Multi-Tier-Transparency)

Competitive Intelligence

This solution enables a deep dive into the target's competitive landscape, including benchmarking against industry peers. Key benefits include:

☐ **Market Position Analysis**: Understanding the target's strengths and weaknesses relative to competitors.

☐ **Opportunity Identification**: Spotting areas where the target could gain a competitive advantage through synergies with the acquiring company.

Here is a Competitive Intelligence example relating to a target company that has Mayun SAS in Columbia as a customer. The intricate and comprehensive details regarding shipments provide valuable insights that can significantly illuminate the competitive positioning of a target company, specifically highlighting Mayun as a significant customer while also emphasizing Nacional de Cobre as a major supplier in the past, which may now be considered a potential merger and acquisition target that is presently at risk, especially as it is being substituted or replaced by the emerging player, Industrias Unidas, in this dynamic market landscape.

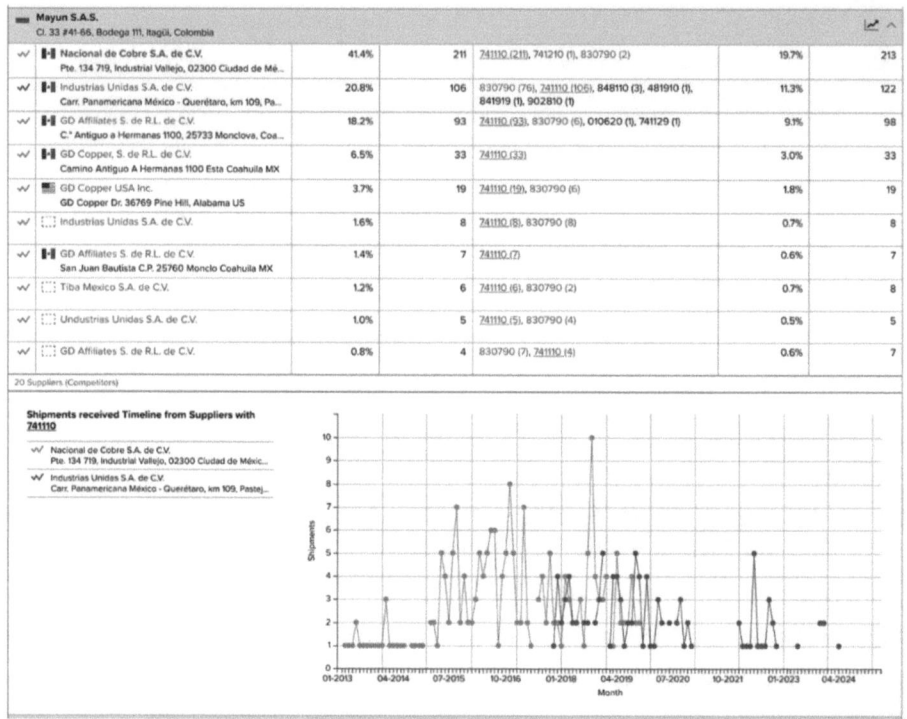

Figure 20: Competitive Intelligence: Shipment details giving insights into the competitive position

 Scan this QR code to view the figure online.

7.4 Conclusion

With ABRAMS world trade wiki, acquirers can conduct a more informed, efficient, and comprehensive due diligence. This enhances the ability to identify risks, validate assumptions, and uncover opportunities that drive successful M&A outcomes.

8. PATEV value for Commercial Due Diligence

Dr.-Ing. Edelbert Häfele, Dr.-Ing. Klaus Illgner-Fehns, Dr.-Ing. Judit Inacsovszky

PATEV Associates GmbH

Figure 21: EY Strategy&Transaction GmbH, Dr. Georg Beckmann: B&I Journey, part 2

In the Due Diligence phase of the M&A process, especially in the Commercial Due Diligence, a detailed value analysis has to be done answering mainly two questions in detail:

❑ How strong is the technological impact of the IP to be aquired on the business of the merged company?

☐ The technological impact can be analyzed by a Deep Dive Analysis in IP and Technology by PATEV "Innovation Intelligence", a Microsoft Power BI application, readable by the management.

☐ What financial value (price tag) has the IP to be acquired?

☐ This Price Tag of the IP Portfolio by PATEV "IP Valuation" is a baseline of the Corporate Value. The Expert Opinion is done according to international Standards like IDW and ISV standards on Patents, Utility models and Know-how, Brands and Design patents.

8.1 PATEV Innovation Intelligence insights: Good or NOT?

Patents can be granted for inventions in all fields of technology. A sophisticated analysis of the patents filed worldwide allows for deep insights into selected industries, market situations, and even some kind of forecast of market development as new patent applications describe current developments mostly before products being launched. "PATEV Innovation Intelligence" is a service supported tool which is designed specifically for such analysis. The unique power lies in its ability to operate on different levels of granularity as it helps to identify markets, analyse specific companies and compare them with other competitors and even drill down to each individual patent which was identified as relevant for the technical field.

Typical industry categories like semiconductors, automotive or chemicals are too broad for a deep analysis. Therefore, the "industry" needs to be narrowed down to a specific technological area. Even this can still be very broad. For detailing the area of interest, the starting point may be a technical area of a specific company but is not restricted to it. Furthermore, it might be of interest to check not only for specific technologies but also for applications for those technologies. There might also be different technical approaches to solve a specific technical problem, it might be different elements which together create a larger entity, like die, bonding, packaging etc. which together create a chip. An example is given in the figure below. Two technological categories have been selected, the frontend side which is structured into three technological groups, and the backend side, again structured into different aspects relevant on the backend side.

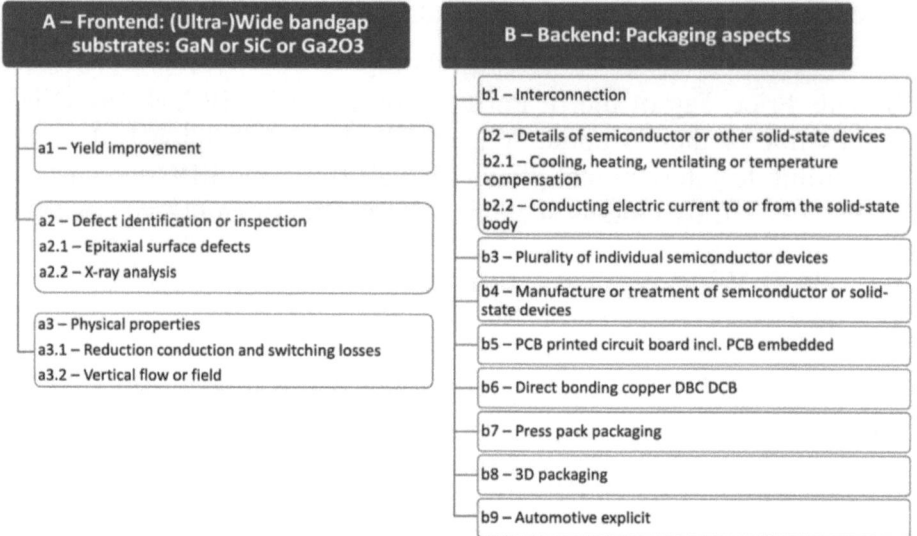

Figure 22: Example of how to structure features of a technology area within an industry. PwC Strategy& - PATEV: Semicon wide-bandgap and packaging innovation analysis, July 2023.

Hierarchical maps are well suited to structure the different related aspects of a technological area. This identification of technologies, areas, applications is key for a successful deep dive analysis. Bottomline, it is important to carefully characterize those terms, in order to optimally guide the query definition and subsequent search in the patent databases.

Once patent literature has been searched and the retrieved information is being processed, an extensive and comprehensive analysis is possible providing a deep market insight. An overview of the patenting activities over time (see next figure) gives an insight into **when** there was a high interest in this domain and when companies spent resources to develop new technologies in the selected field. A sharp increase indicates that companies identified this area as very important while a decrease signals that the relevance of the field goes down. There are several takeaways from this information. If the increase in patenting activities is very recent[4], it means that there is high expectation in future business. If the technology area might affect the company under investigation, you should check the positioning of the company in this field. Maybe it is a good point in time to buy another company which is very active, just because our company has no resources, only little knowledge or simply is too late in the development.

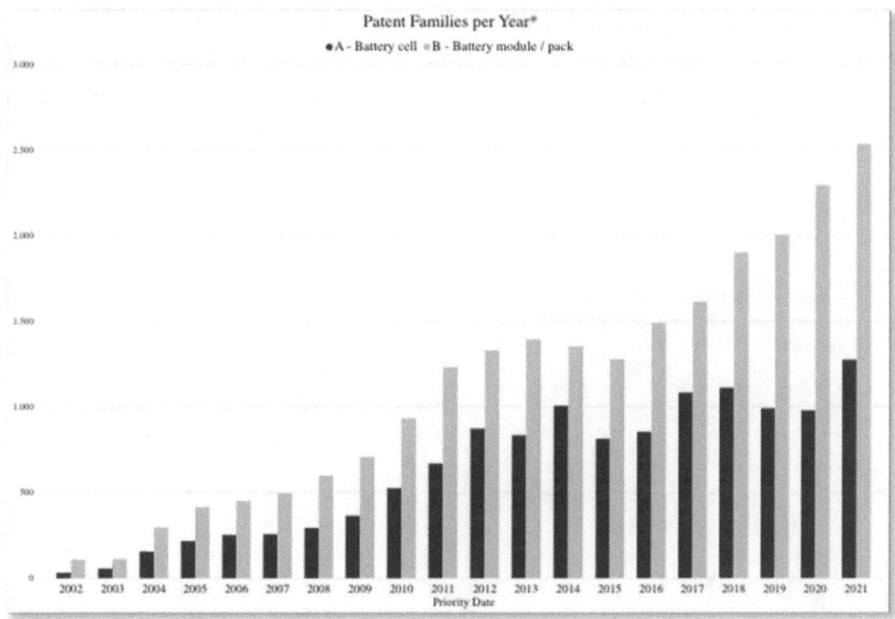

Figure 23: Patenting activities as number of filed patent families (priority: first filing) per year in the selected technology areas. PwC Strategy& - PATEV: EV Battery Innovation analysis, November 2022.

However, a decline in activity does not mean that the technology has lost its relevance. Rather, it may be time to check whether the expectation that the technology was developed has been realized in the marketplace, i.e. whether products based on the patents have entered the market. Although companies usually file patents during technology and product developments, there is no guarantee that a strong portfolio correlates directly to a strong product portfolio and market position. So, it

---

[4] Patent applications are usually published 18 months after filing.

might be time for consolidating portfolios. Companies may want to sell their portfolio because they failed to get traction in a market or want to find partners with complementary portfolios to secure or enlarge their market.

"PATEV Innovation Intelligence" reveals the companies that are active in this area. The most relevant companies are those which have filed the largest number of patent families compared to other companies active in the field (figure below). Filing patents is costly, so for the respective companies this technology is of high commercial importance. At the same time, it demonstrates a high level of competence.

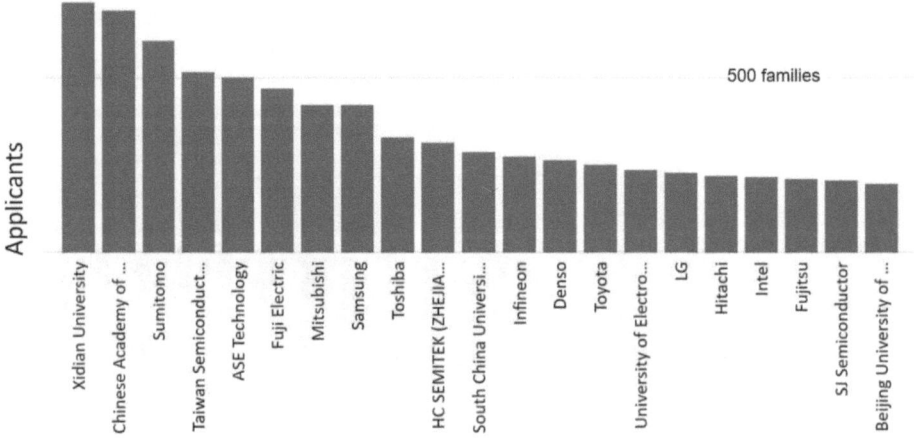

Figure 24: Top applicants in a technology field rated over the number of patent families. PwC Strategy& - PATEV: Semicon wide-bandgap and packaging innovation analysis, July 2023.

There is one more important market insight. Over how many companies are most patents distributed? A very diverse field could be interpreted as it is relatively easy to get into this technical area. When many companies are working in the same field while each of them must differentiate[5] from the others, there is a high likelihood that there is a high

---

[5] A patent application is evaluated by the patent office for its novelty, inventive step and industrial applicability

number of quite specific[6] patents. In contrast it could also be seen that only a few companies filed most of the patents, hence these companies are the key players in this technology area.

A patent family is a set of patents filed in different countries for the same invention. The distribution of patents across countries provides further insights as it reveals which regions are the commercially most interesting. More important patents are usually filed in those countries where products are manufactured and / or sold or in case of recent developments where those markets are expected. In the example below China has by the far the biggest share in patent coverage which attributes to the fact that China is both an important market and at the same time an important manufacturer. The technology under investigation in the example is for instance relevant for e-mobility. At the same time, it is revealed that Europe does not play a relevant role in this domain.

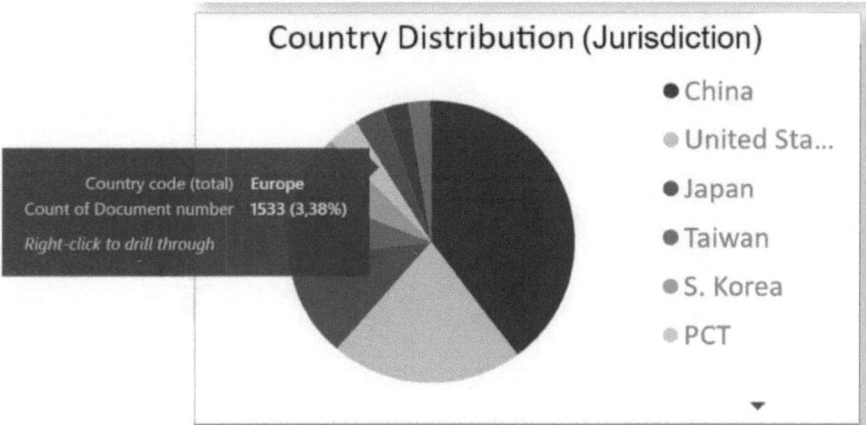

Figure 25: Geographical distribution of patents. PwC Strategy& - PATEV: EV Battery Innovation analysis, November 2022.

The absolute number of patents is only one important dimension. There are patents which obviously cover a fundamental technical element, while there are also patents which are very specific and address a technical niche. To really understand the company's IP portfolio from an M&A perspective it is important to know the relevance of the patents

---

[6] Narrow protection scope

in its portfolio. If a patent is of high relevance, it will frequently be cited by other, later applications. The forward citation, very similar to the citation index in the scientific literature, is a reliable indicator for the relevance of a patent. The diagram generated by PATEV Innovation Intelligence (next figure) shows average numbers for the patent relevance. A high or low patent relevance represents high or low relevance of the entire portfolio. When looking into the company relevance there is another criterion: the intensity of development or how much the company focuses on the subject. A suitable indicator is the relation of patent filings in a certain recent time frame to the total number of patents filed by that company in that technology area. Combining this criterion termed "innovation speed" with the forward citation index creates a very instructive diagram.

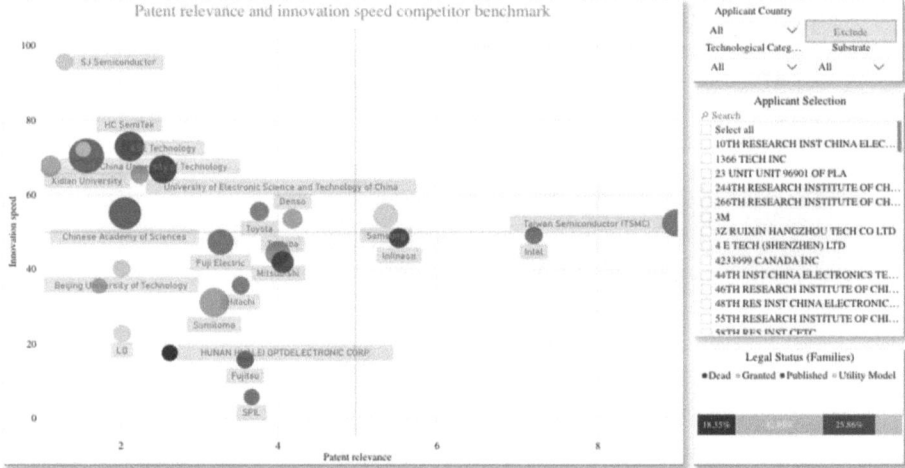

Figure 26: Performance analysis in selected technological categories

It can be read somehow like a SWOT-diagram. Companies with a high innovation speed and high patent relevance appear in the top right corner, while companies with little focus (low innovation speed) and low patent relevance appear in the lower left corner. The radius of the circle indicates the number of patent families filed by that company in the technology area under investigation. In this example well known large companies lead in terms of relevance. However, this might not be always the case, as in this analysis small companies can show up with a high relevance, which will not have been identified by just looking at the sheer number of patent families. Those companies with relevant patents, often having only a small portfolio, can be of high interest for M&A.

So far, the analysis was on the technology area in total. Nevertheless, the specification of the features at the beginning was more detailed. For a more detailed view, the complete analysis as described up to now can be done also on individual feature categories (e.g. A and / or B). Listing the number of patents per individual feature reveals in more detail what the company is really focusing on in a specific field (next figure)[7]. In this example ASE Technology for instance has no activities in the frontend (category A) while it has substantial activities in the category B (backend). This so-called "White Space Analysis" makes areas with little or even no activity apparent. In contrast, Sumitomo focuses mostly on frontend with very little activities in the backend. Assuming Sumitomo would like to strengthen its position also in category B, then this analysis of the patent distribution over the features would indicate that a combination of Sumitomo with ASE Technology would create a very powerful portfolio. Also, direct competitors can be identified which work on the same technology area and feature, like Fuji Electric and Mitsubishi. A check back on relevance (see figure before) shows also similar positions in average.

---

[7] The numbers cannot be added, as patents may match several features and counted for each feature.

Heat-Map (Competitor Analysis)

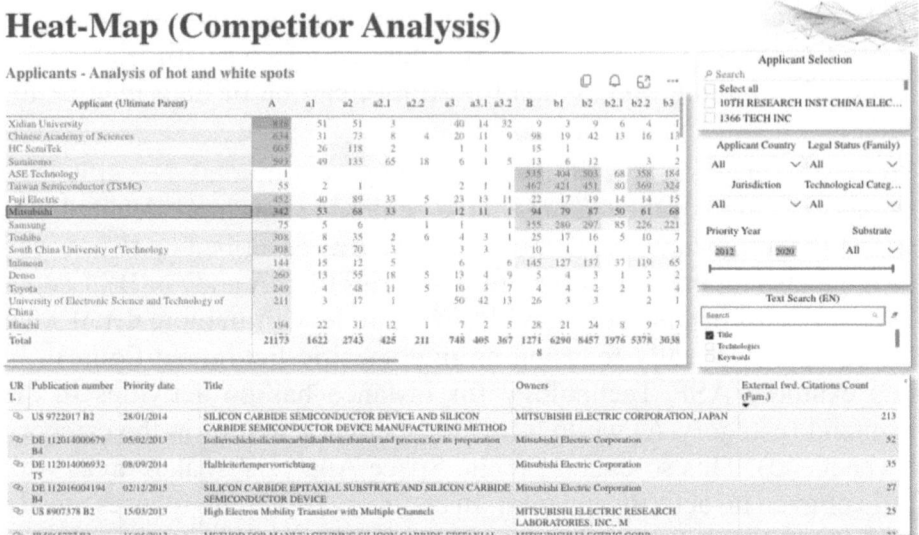

Figure 27: Competitor heatmap as a listing of patenting activities for each individual feature. PwC Strategy& - PATEV: Semicon wide-bandgap and packaging innovation analysis, July 2023.

Furthermore, PATEV Innovation Intelligence allows to drill down into the individual patent families and patents. Here, it becomes apparent that Fuji's most relevant patent family has a citation count of 50 while Mitsubishi has a patent family in this field with a forward citation count of 213.

So far only individual features have been analyzed. At the same time patents may apply to several features. Correlating two features brings new insights regarding the coverage. In the example shown below there is a high correlation between the features in category B whereas in category A there are even some white spaces. White spaces indicate that there is no patent covering both aspects. As an intelligent combination of features may fulfil the novelty criterion, such white spaces signal potential for new applications. Obviously not all combinations are sensible. From an M&A perspective this view on the portfolio could signal additional market potential by addressing those white spots.

Heat-Map (Technology Analysis)

Technology Focus - Analysis of hot and white spots

Feature	A	a1	a2	a2.1	a2.2	a3	a3.1	a3.2	B	b1	b2	b2.1	b2.2	b3
A - Frontend: (Ultra-)Wide bandgap substrates: GaN or SiC or Ga2O3	21630	1649	2791	428	218	769	412	381	604	237	376	175	189	190
a1 - Yield improvement	1649	1649	335	96	35	50	18	32	59	29	35	6	18	18
a2 - Defect identification or inspection	2791	335	2791	428	218	69	33	37	37	12	15	4	9	10
a2.1 - epitaxial surface defects	428	96	428	428	7	13	4	9						
a2.2 - X-ray analysis	218	35	218	7	218	5		5	3	2				
a3 - Physical properties	769	50	69	13	5	769	412	381	27	13	17	9	14	11
a3.1 - Reduction conduction and switching losses	412	18	33	4		412	412	24	14	6	9	3	7	8
a3.2 - Vertical flow or field	381	32	37	9	5	381	24	381	13	7	8	6	7	3
B - Backend: Packaging aspects	604	59	37		3	27	14	13	12781	6311	8497	1985	5399	3049
b1 - interconnection	237	29	12		2	13	6	7	6311	6311	5774	1141	4491	2370
b2 - details of semiconductor or other solid state devices	376	35	15			17	9	8	8497	5774	8497	1985	5399	2676
b2.1 - cooling, heating, ventilating or temperature compensation	175	6	4			9	3	6	1985	1141	1985	1985	1067	695
b2.2 - conducting electric current to or from the solid state body	189	18	9			14	7	7	5399	4491	5399	1067	5399	2008
b3 - plurality of individual semiconductor devices	190	18	10			11	8	3	3049	2370	2676	695	2008	3049
b4 - manufacture or treatment of semiconductor or solid state devices	267	40	17	1		15	9	6	7477	4323	4963	886	3405	1842
b5 - PCB printed circuit board inc. PCB embedded	128	11	9			7	2	5	3467	2406	2901	706	2069	1358
b6 - direct bonding copper DBC DCB	64	6	3			3	2	1	292	182	265	166	180	122
b7 - press pack packaging	2								20	6	13	2	7	6
Total	21630	1649	2791	428	218	769	412	381	12781	6311	8497	1985	5399	3049

Figure 28: Technology Heatmap visualizing correlations between two technology features. PwC Strategy& - PATEV: Semicon wide-bandgap and packaging innovation analysis, July 2023.

The analysis of filed patent applications provides a powerful tool to get insights into the market situation in a specific technology area and the position of companies in this area. Answers to the following questions can be found:

❏ Who is leading the development in a certain technology area / product or applications?

❏ What is the strength of a company in a certain technical field?

❏ Who are key competitors?

❏ When did relevant developments happen?

❏ Who has made relevant developments?

❏ Where are technical gaps in the coverage?

❏ Which are the most active geographical regions?

❏ What is the innovation speed?

❏ How relevant are the patents?

❏ Are there any hidden champions?

Relating to M&A, the answers to these questions could help

❏ to pick the right company with the best IP fit

❏ to find hidden champions

❏ open up new dimensions for M&A success

8.2 Valuation of IP Assets: Real Value or Substantial Risk?

In the due diligence phase, a key step in the M&A process is valuation. IP can represent a significant part of the company's value, up to 90%. The focus should therefore be on IP valuation.

In M&A and other occasions, there are four applications of the valuation of IP. The following figure is a schematic representation and grouping of these occasions.

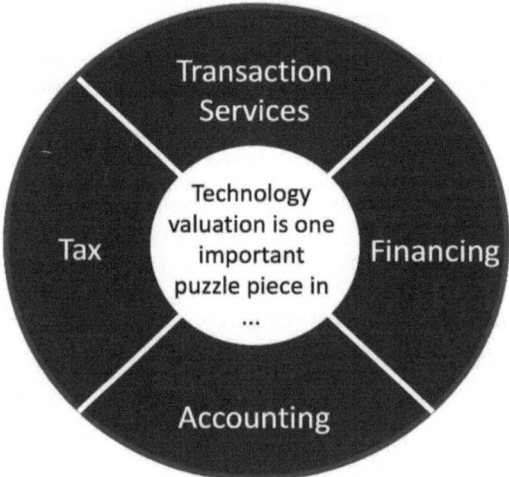

Figure 29: Main applications for IP valuation

The following is a detailed list of valuation situations - all of which can be solved by a PATEV valuation service using IP analysis tools, sometimes in cooperation with advisors and consulting companies.

Transaction services

Typical transactional situations include Mergers, Acquisitions, Corporate/Business Transactions, Licensing and Technology Transfer.

M&A: Valuation is needed to assess the fair market value of IP assets for negotiation, pricing and integration planning. Proper IP valuation prevents buyers from overpaying or overlooking hidden IP value. Some IP rights, such as licenses, may not be transferable, affecting post-merger integration. Part of the M&A process is determining strategic fit -

assessing how the acquired IP fits with the buyer's existing portfolio and business strategy. In addition, an IP valuation helps to forecast the revenue potential of the acquired IP.

In an M&A journey, valuation can play a role in several steps of the process:

- Due Diligence prior to an acquisition: Before acquiring a company, the acquirer conducts due diligence to evaluate the target's assets, including its IP portfolio. The objective is to identify and evaluate the quality, scope and financial value of the target's IP assets to ensure that they are aligned with the acquirer's strategic objectives and do not present significant risks.

- Negotiation and pricing: During the negotiation phase, both parties must agree on the value of the target company, including its IP assets.

- Especially in IP and Know-how driven deals the collaboration with STIFEL Investmentbank[8] has shown a clear relevance of IP Valuation, in Business Cases where the Business Value based on Profits was not an option. Even with no Profit but a clear Value Proposition based on technological leadership has shown up with high revenues in the transaction.

- Financing and investment decisions: Acquirers may need to value IP assets in order to secure financing or attract investors for the acquisition. They need to demonstrate the value of IP assets to lenders or investors to ensure adequate financing for the transaction.

- Valuation for Purchase Price Allocation (PPA): After the acquisition, the purchase price must be allocated to the acquired assets, including IP, for financial reporting and tax purposes.

- Post-Merger Integration (PMI): After the acquisition, the acquirer integrates the target's IP assets into its existing portfolio. The valuation is necessary to assess the value and strategic fit of the acquired IP, to ensure effective integration and to maximise synergies.

---

[8] **Dr. Bernd Schneider**, Managing Director STIFEL, Office Frankfurt

Corporate/Business Transactions: IP valuation is often required in various corporate transactions, including spin-offs, IPOs, divestitures and restructurings. It is necessary to assess the value of the IP assets involved in the transaction and to ensure fair treatment of all parties. Valuation can help identify and sell off unused or under-utilized IP assets.

Licensing: IP owners may wish to monetize patents, trademarks or, for example, copyrights through licensing deals. When licensing IP to third parties, it is essential to determine appropriate royalty rates and license fees. When negotiating licensing agreements, a fair License Fee determination ensures that both parties enter into a fair and profitable agreement.

Technology transfer: Universities, research institutions and companies may value IP for technology transfer and commercialization purposes. Licensing, spin-offs or technological partnerships are common opportunities.

Finance

Startups and other R&D-intensive companies seeking investment often need to value their IP to attract investors or secure financing. Companies may use their IP Assets in Financial Engineering. A credible valuation can enhance the ability to attract investors or obtain loans. The purpose is therefore to demonstrate the value of IP assets to potential investors or lenders. Studies show that patent and trademark applications are real funding boosters. [9] [10]

IP based financing in leasing structures like Sale and Licensing Back (SLB):

---

[9] European Patent Office and European Union Intellectual Property Office, "Patents, trade marks and startup finance: Funding and exit performance of European startups," Oct. 2023. [Online]. Available: https://link.epo.org/web/publications/studies/en-patents-trade-marks-and-startup-finance-study.pdf (accessed Jan. 31, 2025).

[10] World Intellectual Property Organization, "Securing Loans with Your IP Assets," Hands-on IP Finance Series, WIPO Publication No. 2011EN, 2024. [Online]. Available: https://www.wipo.int/edocs/pubdocs/en/wipo-pub-2011-en-securing-loans-with-your-ip-assets.pdf. [Accessed: Jan. 31, 2025].

Using IP Sale and Licensing Back structures in Financial Engineering is well known in US and is more and more used in Europe, too. Doing so, the IP Assets (brands or patents) are bought by the Buyer, a Specific Purpose Vehicle PPV. So the Company gets money for its secret reserves. For further use of these IP Assets the company pays monthly license fees. At the end of the agreement, often after 5 years, the IP Assets are transferred back to the company, the former owner.

Venture capital and private equity decisions: Investors assess the IP portfolio before committing capital. Startups and growth stage companies often rely on their IP portfolio to attract venture capital (VC) or private equity (PE) investors. Investors need to understand the value of the company's IP to assess its potential for generating future revenues and competitive advantages.

Debt Financing: Debt advisory is getting more and more important in Corporate Finance[11]

Debt Funds require a reliable valuation of IP assets before accepting them as a key value in the Financing Structure.

Initial Public Offerings (IPOs): Companies preparing for an IPO must disclose the value of their IP assets in their prospectus to attract public investors. IP valuation helps to establish the company's overall valuation and demonstrates the strength of its intangible assets to potential shareholders. IP valuation helps to justify the investment by demonstrating the value of the company's innovations and their market potential.

Reverse IPO: An intermediate solution between a direct listing and a traditional IPO: going public quickly through a shell company (reverse IPO, reverse merger, cold IPO, shell purchase)[12].

---

[11] **Peer Macketanz,** Director Capital & Debt Advisory | Transactions & Corporate Finance (TCF), EY-Parthenon GmbH Wirtschaftsprüfungsgesellschaft

[12] **Werner Weiss,** Managing Director Yggdrasil Bridge Finance GmbH, CEO Yggdrasil SPAC 1 AG, www.IPO-Mantelgesellschaft.de

Raising Funds for R&D and Innovation: Companies seeking funding for research and development (R&D) or innovation projects can use their existing IP portfolio to demonstrate their potential for future growth.

Bankruptcy, Insolvency: In bankruptcy proceedings, IP assets may need to be valued for liquidation or reorganization purposes. If a company goes bankrupt, its valuable IP assets can be a solution element in planning the future. Companies in financial distress may re-evaluate the IP to attract potential buyers. The value of IP assets is determined for creditors, stakeholders, and legal proceedings[13].

Accounting

In financial reporting and accounting companies need to report the value of their IP assets in financial statements for compliance with accounting standards (e.g., IFRS, GAAP). Valuation ensures accurate financial reporting and compliance with regulatory requirements. Determining fair market value is essential for accurately reporting assets on the balance sheet.

Financial Reporting and Capital increase: Companies are required to report the value of their IP assets in financial statements according to accounting standards such as International Financial Reporting Standards (IFRS) and Generally Accepted Accounting Principles (GAAP) or German Commercial Code (HGB).

Especially when IP Assets from one of the shareholders are used in the context of an increase of capital ("Capital Replacement") a reliable value of the IP Assets is a basic need.

Goodwill allocation / Purchase Price Allocation: When a company acquires another, part of the purchase price may be attributed to intangible assets, thereby affecting goodwill in the financial statements. After a business combination (e.g., merger or acquisition), the purchase

---

[13] **Markus Fröhlich,** Owner, Attorney, Certified Restructuring and Restructuring Manager, Specialist Attorney for Restructuring and Insolvency Law, FROEHLICH Lawyers Insolvency Administrators Tax Advisors

price must be allocated to the acquired assets, including IP, to ensure accurate financial reporting.

Impairment Test: Companies must periodically test their IP assets for impairment to ensure that their carrying value does not exceed their recoverable amount, i.e. they must identify and account for any decline in the value of IP assets, to ensure accurate financial statements.

Amortization of IP Assets: IP assets with finite useful lives must be amortized over their expected lives in order to allocate the cost of IP assets over their useful lives and reflect their consumption in the financial statements.

Internal and External Audits: Auditors may require IP valuation to verify the accuracy of financial statements and ensure compliance with accounting standards.

Tax Planning and Compliance

Valuation of IP is required for tax purposes, including transfer pricing, capital gains tax, tax amortization benefits and determining tax liabilities on asset transfers. The purpose is to determine the taxable value of IP assets and to ensure compliance with tax regulations. Incorrect IP valuation can lead to tax audits and penalties for mispricing. Governments may also offer tax incentives for R&D investments, which require accurate IP valuation.

Compliance with International Tax Laws: Governments require fair valuation of IP to prevent tax evasion.

Avoidance of Double Taxation Issues: Ensures fair taxation when IP is transferred between jurisdictions.

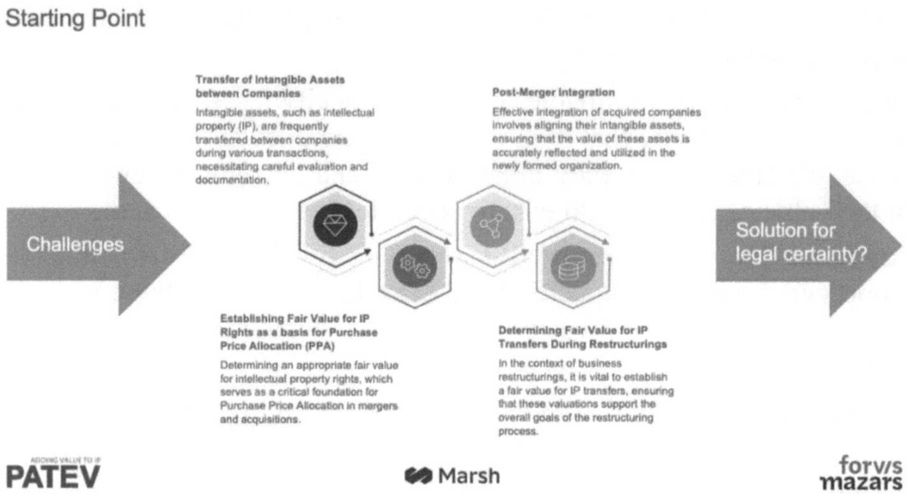

Starting Point

Figure 30: Forvis Mazars: Reducing TP Risks and Improving Legal Certainty, Webcast Forvis Mazars – PATEV – Marsh, March 2025.

Transfer Pricing: Multinational enterprises need to value IP when transferring it between related entities in different tax jurisdictions, to ensure that the transfer price reflects the arm's length principle, as required by tax authorities, and to avoid penalties for non-compliance.

Capital Gains Tax: When IP assets are sold or transferred, the capital gains tax liability must be calculated based on the difference between the sale price and the asset's tax basis. The valuation purpose is to determine the taxable gain or loss and to ensure accurate tax reporting.

Tax Amortization Benefits (TAB): Companies can amortize the cost of IP assets over their useful lives for tax purposes, thereby reducing taxable income. It is therefore necessary to calculate the tax benefits associated with the amortization of IP assets.

When Insurance can be a Solution for TP Issues? **03**

Tax insurance can be useful in the following circumstances:

M&A transactions	**Corporate restructuring**	**Winding-up of fund structures**	**Balance sheet protections**
• Known historical tax risks. • Tax consequences of a change of ownership.	• Corporate spin-offs or mergers. • **Alternative for a binding ruling.**	• Repatriation of profits. • Insolvency proceedings. • Clean exit. • Latent tax liabilities.	• Transfer of tax risk from balance sheet to insurer. • Equity and cash flow relief.

 PATEV   ● Marsh   forvis mazars

Figure 31: Marsh: Tax Insurance, Webcast Forvis Mazars – PATEV – Marsh, March 2025.

Tax Reporting for IP Holding Companies: Companies that hold IP assets in separate entities (e.g., IP holding companies) need to value their IP for tax reporting purposes.

Other tax reporting purposes include tax deductions for R&D expenses, related to the creation of IP or withholding tax on royalties, when IP is licensed to foreign entities.

Other occasions

Here is an overview of other occasions for IP valuation:

Litigation and Dispute Resolution: In cases of intellectual property infringement, breach of contract, or ownership disputes, valuation is required to quantify damages or settlements.

Investor Relationship: Investors of public companies are looking for investments with a positive development of value. There, one indicator of a solid investment, especially in Life Science companies, is the Value of the activated IP Assets in the balance sheet.

Strategic planning and management: Companies may value their IP as a baseline for strategic decisions, such as R&D investment, market entry, or portfolio management. The goal is to align IP strategy with business objectives and optimize the value of IP assets.

Joint Ventures and Partnerships/Strategic Alliances: When forming joint ventures or partnerships, the IP assets contributed by each party need to be valued, to ensure equitable contributions and fair sharing of profits or losses. Valuation can also determine the value of IP assets when the joint venture is dissolved.

Insurance: Companies may seek to insure their high valuable IP assets against risks such as infringement, theft, or damage. The goal is to determine the appropriate coverage and premiums for IP insurance policies.

Research and Development: Companies may wish to value their IP to prioritize R&D projects or assess the potential return on investment for new innovations. They want to allocate resources effectively and maximize the value of their R&D efforts.

By understanding these detailed reasons for IP valuation, companies can make informed financial, legal, and strategic decisions in different business contexts.

PATEV's New Value services offer solutions for all these different valuation situations.

PATEV applies valuation methods that are particularly in line with the activities of standardization communities (IDW S5[14], DIN/ISO[15], IVS 210[16]).

---

[14] IDW (German Institute of Public Auditors) Section 5: "Guidelines for measuring intangible assets", introduced by the Technical Committee for Business Valuations and Commerce (FAUB), latest version 16.04.2015 [online] Available at: https://www.idw.de/idw/verlautbarungen/idw-s-5/43024 [Accessed 31 Jan. 2025].

[15] DIN ISO 10668 Brand valuation - Requirements for monetary brand valuation (ISO/FDIS 10668) 2011

[16] International Valuation Standards Council, IVS 210 Intangible Assets, Effective 31 January 2020. Pp 63-79: IVS 210 Intangible Assets, [online] Available at: https://www.ivsc.org/new-edition-of-the-international-valuation-standards-ivs-published/; https://www.appraisers.org/docs/default-source/5---standards/ivs-effective-

The valuation method is determined by the purpose of the valuation.

The first step is to assign the purpose of the valuation to one of the two valuation concepts: value in use or transfer value. In both cases three concepts are applicable as defined in the standard IDW S5.

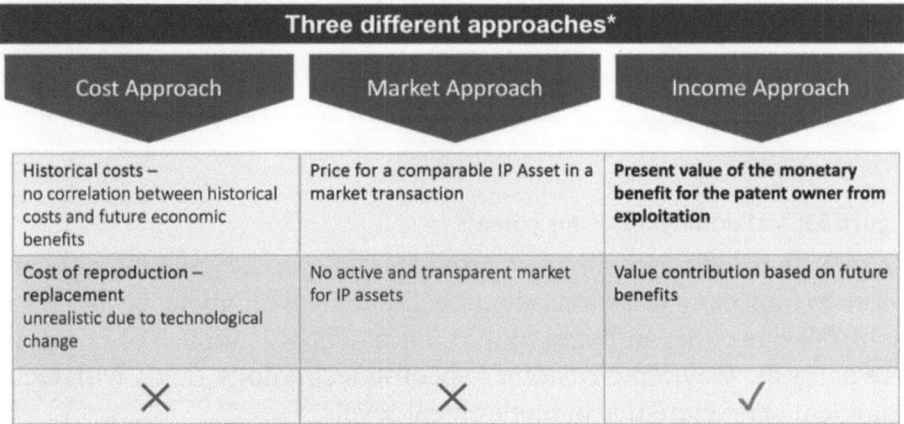

Figure 32: Basic valuation approaches

In most cases, the license analogy method is chosen. The effective royalty rate is the most value-driving parameter. Even if the royalty rates of similar business cases are well known in the literature, these baseline royalty rates still need to be adapted to the unique technological business case. In the case of patents, the following 10 specific factors need to be considered.

In the case of patents, a key valuation criterion is the patent position of the company or business unit in the competitive environment. Innovative strength alone does not guarantee a company's success - just as intelligent analysis tools do not automatically generate added value.

31-january-2025-redline-edition-33-51.pdf?sfvrsn=d768966b_1 [Accessed 31 Jan. 2025].

Patent-related	Technological	Competition-relevant
Legal status – based on patent register citations or in cooperation with a patent attorney	Technological cohesion	Level of technological competition
Bypassing potential – substitution solutions (from patent search and market competition perspective)	Forward & backward citations	Characteristic intensity in the competitive environment
Enforceability aspects – based on client information or in cooperation with a patent attorney	Product & process correlation	
Maximum possible remaining term	Technological competence	

Figure 33: Valuation factors for patents

PATEV Innovation Intelligence provides transparency and the right answers to important questions about technological competence and leadership. We use this software tool in our patent valuation. For competitive analysis, we define customer-specific technology fields with technological characteristics in hierarchical levels.

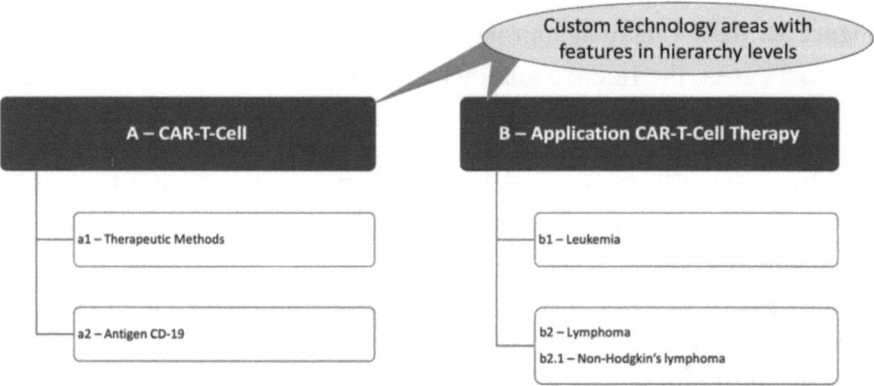

Figure 34: Customer-Specific technology fields and characteristics for patent search and analysis

The following figure shows a heatmap of a competitive analysis, with the abbreviations A, a1-a2, B, b1-b2-b2.1 for the technological structuring and hierarchical levels of characteristics.

Known competitors in the market or TOP applicants in the custom technology areas and characteristics.

	A	a1	a2	B	b1	b2	b2.1	Gesamt
University of Pennsylvania	153	76	18	10	9	2		153
US Health and Human Services (HHS)	142	57	9	9	6	4	1	142
University of California	121	42	3					121
Novartis	110	58	15	7	5	2	1	110
JUNO THERAPEUTICS INC	105	67	7	13	7	10	7	105
Memorial Sloan Kettering Cancer Center	89	35	5	9	6	4	1	89
AUTOLUS LIMITED	84	18	3	5	4	2		84
SHENZHEN BINDE BIO TECH CO LTD & ...	74	8	10					74
Cellectis	69	42	4	11	9	9		69
Fred Hutchinson Cancer Research Center	63	24	4	5	5	3	1	63
Dana-Farber Cancer Insititute	60	18		2	1	1		60
University of Texas	58	32	1	1	1			58
SHANGHAI HRAIN BIOTECHNOLOGY CO LTD & ...	53	7	17	5	4	5		53
Inserm	48	21		2	1	1		48
Hope City	47	24	4	5	2	3		47
Baylor College of Medicine	46	30	2	2	2			46
Massachusetts General Hospital	44	20	3					44
SHANGHAI CELL THERAPY ENGINEERING TECHNOLOGY RES CT CO LTD & ...	44	12	2					44
Gesamt	6015	2411	375	238	141	140	24	6015

Figure 35: Valuation Report, Heatmap – competitive environment,

Screenshot PATEV Innovation Intelligence, Showcase Life Science CAR T-CELL

The valuation is individual, yet transparent, efficient and reliable. Within our proven track record, more than 2000 valuation related projects have been successfully realized in many industries in a broad and international range of applications.

9. Disruptive automation of Post Merger Integration

Dr. Karl Michael Popp

Post merger integration is a high-effort, complex process with many dependencies between the different tasks. In this section we present a subset of all integration tasks that apply to the tools and scenarios in the book. Full coverage of merger integration will be available in an upcoming book [Popp,25].

9.1 Task Synergy Implementation and Control

Task description

During the process of merger integration, the elements of synergy implementation and control are paramount in ensuring the efficacy of the integrated organization. Synergy pertains to the identification and utilization of the collective strengths of the merging entities to generate enhanced value that surpasses what they could attain in isolation. This endeavor commences with a comprehensive assessment of prospective synergies, including but not limited to cost reductions, revenue increases, and operational efficiencies. Implementation necessitates a methodical strategy, which encompasses the formulation of a thorough integration blueprint that delineates principal objectives, timelines, and designated responsibilities. Robust control mechanisms are indispensable for tracking progress, mitigating risks, and assuring that the integration adheres to its intended course. Frequent performance evaluations and modifications to the integration plan are instrumental in addressing any arising challenges while seizing new opportunities. Communication and collaboration across all strata of the organization are crucial for sustaining alignment and dedication to the integration objectives. Ultimately, the successful realization of synergy and effective control during the merger integration process is instrumental in fostering long-term value creation and establishing a competitive edge.

Attributes of the Task

The task is a decision task.

The task problem is structured.

The task has the following goal(s):

☐ Synergy: realized

The task has the following objectives:

☐ Synergy: maximized

The task consists of the following actions

☐ Confirm and prioritize the synergies identified during the due diligence phase

☐ Validate the feasibility of capturing these synergies

☐ Establish KPIs to track synergy realization

☐ Implement regular reporting mechanisms to monitor progress

☐ Monitor the execution of the plan

The task works on the following data object types, among others:

Synergy, Synergy plan, Integration project, Integration project plan, Business plan

Automatability

This task is not automatable.

9.2 Task Production integration

Task description

Integration of production facilities during a merger is a complex task that requires meticulous planning and execution. The process begins with a thorough assessment of the existing facilities of both companies to identify redundancies and opportunities for optimization. Key activities include aligning production processes, standardizing equipment, and ensuring compatibility of technology systems. This integration aims to enhance operational efficiency and reduce costs by consolidating resources and streamlining workflows. Effective communication and collaboration between teams are essential to address any cultural and operational differences. Additionally, managing the transition of personnel and maintaining morale is crucial to ensure smooth integration. Continuous monitoring and adjustment of the integration plan based on performance metrics help in achieving the desired outcomes. Ultimately, successful integration of production facilities supports the strategic goals of the merger, driving value creation and competitive advantage.

Attributes of the Task

The task problem is structured.

The task consists of the following actions

- ☐ Assess the production capabilities, processes, and technologies of both companies
- ☐ Determine how the production systems, technologies, and processes of both companies align with each other
- ☐ Create a detailed plan for integrating the production systems, including timelines, responsibilities
- ☐ Ensure that the integrated production capabilities support the overall business strategy and objectives
- ☐ Identify and implement best practices from both companies to standardize production processes
- ☐ Leverage new technologies and innovations to enhance production capabilities
- ☐ Provide training and support to ensure a smooth transition/integration of production processes
- ☐ Continuously monitor the integrated production systems to identify areas for further optimization

The task works on the following data object types, among others:

Production of NewCo, Analytical applications of NewCo production, Production application system of NewCo, Production capacity of NewCo, Production costs of NewCo, Shipping of NewCo production, Shipping application of NewCo production, Maintenance of the NewCo production facilities, Maintenance application of the NewCo production facilities, Operations of NewCo Production, Performance of NewCo Production, Production process of NewCo, Section of the NewCo production process, NewCo production quality, Quality application of NewCo production, NewCo production resource management, NewCo production resource management application, Risk of NewCo production, Parts tracking in NewCo production, Parts tracking application on the NewCo shop floor, Operations of the target production, Production capacity of the target, Analytical applications of production, Maintenance of production facilities, Quality of target production, Production process of the target, Section of the target production process, Production plan of the target, Performance of the target production, Production site of the target company, Shift schedule of the target, Assignment of NewCo workers to segments, Worker of NewCo, Assignment of workers to segments, Worker of the target

Automatability

This task is partially automatable.

9.3 Task GTM integration

Task description

The integration of go-to-market strategies during a merger represents a pivotal undertaking that necessitates the alignment of the marketing and sales methodologies of the entities involved to optimize revenue generation capabilities. This undertaking commences with a thorough examination of the market positioning, customer demographics, and competitive environments of both organizations. The objective is to discern synergies and formulate a cohesive strategy that capitalizes on the strengths inherent in both organizations. Fundamental activities encompass the harmonization of branding, the alignment of product portfolios, and the integration of sales teams to ensure a unified market approach. The efficacy of communication and strategic change management is paramount to navigating cultural disparities and facilitating a seamless transition. Furthermore, the ongoing evaluation and modification of the strategy in response to market feedback are vital for realizing the intended objectives. Ultimately, successful integration of go-to-market strategies significantly enhances customer experience and propels growth within the newly established organization.

Attributes of the Task

The task is a decision task.

The task problem is structured.

The task has the following goal(s):

❒ Draft GTM integration plan: executed

❒ Operations of NewCo GTM activities: prepared

The task has the following objectives:

❒ Risk of NewCo Go-To-Market: minimized

❒ GTM synergy: maximized

The task consists of the following actions

❒ Conduct a thorough analysis of the target market to understand customer needs, preferences, and competitive landscape. is automated by 1 tool(s).

❒ Align the products or services of both companies to create a cohesive offering that meets the needs of the target market

❒ Integrate sales and marketing strategies to ensure consistent messaging, branding, and customer engagement. is automated by 1 tool(s).

❒ Identify overlaps and integrate customer bases is automated by 1 tool(s).

❒ Evaluate and integrate distribution channels to optimize reach and efficiency in delivering products or services to customers

❒ Evaluate and integrate partner models and programs is not automated.

☐ Focus on enhancing the customer experience by optimizing GTM processes, improving service quality, and addressing feedback

☐ Establish key performance indicators (KPIs) to track the success of the go-to-market integration

The task works on the following data object types, among others:

GTM costs of NewCo, GTM model of NewCo, Operations of NewCo GTM activities, GTM costs of the target, Operations of the target GTM activities, GTM model of the buyer, Draft GTM integration plan, GTM model of the target, Contracts for NewCo NewCo GTM processes, Risk of NewCo Go-To-Market, Legal aspect of the GTM Application Contract, Target GTM processes, GTM applications of the target, Contracts for target GTM applications, Costs for target GTM applications, Target go-to-market risk, GTM synergy, Complementarity of the GTM model

Automatability

This task is partially automatable.

9.4   Task Finance integration

Task description

Finance integration during a merger encompasses the alignment of the financial operations and systems of the entities to guarantee a cohesive transition. This endeavor entails the consolidation of financial statements, the harmonization of accounting methodologies, and the integration of financial reporting systems. It necessitates a comprehensive examination of both companies' financial architectures to discern synergies and prospective cost efficiencies. Furthermore, finance integration encompasses the administration of cash flow, the alignment of budgets, and the assurance of compliance with regulatory stipulations. Effective communication and collaboration among finance teams are imperative to rectify any discrepancies and to uphold financial stability. Ultimately, successful finance integration

> bolsters the overarching strategic objectives of the merger, augmenting value creation for stakeholders.

Attributes of the Task

The task is a decision task.

The task problem is structured.

The task has the following goal(s):

❏ Financial processes of NewCo: aligned

The task has the following objectives:

❏ Target business: continued

The task consists of the following actions

❏ Ensure that accounting practices, policies, and reporting standards are aligned

❏ Combine financial statements to reflect the merged entity's financial position accurately

❏ Align budgeting and planning processes for the merged entity

❏ Combine tax strategies to optimize tax efficiency and compliance

❏ Integrate financial operations and reporting systems and software

❏ Develop a strategy to manage cash flow effectively

❏ Identify opportunities to optimize working capital and improve liquidity

❏ Evaluate and mitigate financial risks

❏ Combine treasury functions to manage cash, investments, and financial risks

❏ Ensure that financial policies are consistent for the merged entity

❏ Keep investors, employees, and other stakeholders informed

❏ Ensure compliance with financial regulations and reporting requirements

❏ Establish key performance indicators (KPIs) to track financial performance

☐ Identify and capitalize on financial synergies to drive growth and profitability

The task works on the following data object types, among others:

Annual reports, Financial position of the buyer, Draft financial integration plan, Draft financing concept, Financial complementarity, Financial synergy, Deal Financing Concept, Costs of the Deal Financing Concept, Tax effect of the financing concept, NewCo accounting guidelines, Annual reports of NewCo, NewCo application of accounting and valuation options, Financial statements, NewCo business registrations and business licenses, Cash flow of NewCo, Profitability of NewCo, NewCo finance department, Financial processes of NewCo, Financial position of NewCo, NewCo control agreements, Profit and Loss Transfer Agreements of NewCo, Shareholder list of NewCo, Management reports of NewCo, Guarantees of NewCo, Trade register extract of NewCo, Working Capital of NewCo, Financial processes of the target, Financial position of the target, Application of accounting and valuation options, NewCo application of accounting and valuation options, NewCo business registrations and business licenses

Automatability

This task is partially automatable.

9.5 Task Target supplier integration

Task description

> This task cares about all integration aspects relating to the multi-tier supplier network of the target into the buyer organization to create the NewCo supplier network. All suppliers are checked for compliance and resilience and supplier-related synergies from alignment of supply_chains between target and buyer are created.

Attributes of the Task

The task is a decision task.

The task problem is structured.

The task has the following goal(s):

☐ Supplier of the target: analyzed

The task has the following objectives:

☐ Buyer-target complementarity: maximized

The task Target supplier integration has the following roles assigned:

☐ Production expert of the buyer
☐ Production expert of the target
☐ Administration expert of the target
☐ Administration expert of the buyer

The task consists of the following actions

☐ Consolidate vendor relationships
☐ Transition of supplier operations
☐ Supplier communication
☐ Supplier risk management and continuity planning

The task works on the following data object types, among others:

Supplier of the target, Vendor contract, Supplier relationship, Supply chain, Material supplier of the target company, Service supplier of the target, Production material of the target company, Target coverage of supply chain, Supply chain complementarity, Supply Chain Synergy, Supplier of the buyer, Buyer coverage of supply chain, NewCo coverage of the supply chain, Supplier of NewCo, Material supplier of NewCo, Supplier relationship of NewCo, Supplier contract of NewCo

Automatability

This task is partially automatable.

9.6 Task Legal integration

Task description

Legal post-merger integration (PMI) refers to the process of aligning the legal structures, obligations, and governance frameworks of two previously independent entities following a merger or acquisition. This phase is crucial for ensuring compliance with regulatory requirements, such as antitrust laws, and for addressing any legal liabilities that may arise from the consolidation. A primary focus of legal PMI is the harmonization of contractual obligations, including employment agreements, supplier contracts, and intellectual property rights, to prevent potential disputes. Furthermore, the integration process involves careful review and restructuring of corporate governance, ensuring that the merged entity operates within the legal confines of its jurisdiction. Legal due diligence during PMI also encompasses the assessment of potential litigation risks, which may affect the financial and operational stability of the combined organization. Ultimately, effective legal post-merger integration helps mitigate risks, facilitates smoother operational transitions, and contributes to the overall success of the merger or acquisition.

Attributes of the Task

The task is a decision task.

The task problem is structured.

The task has the following goal(s):

❏ Draft Legal Integration Plan: executed

❏ Legal aspect: executed

The task has the following objectives:

❏ Target business: continued

❏ Integration success: maximized

❏ Risk: minimized

The task has the following subtasks

❏ Tax integration

❐ IP integration

The task works on the following data object types, among others:

Draft Legal Integration Plan, Legal aspect of a NewCo brand or trademark, Legal aspect of NewCo taxes, Legal aspect of a NewCo customer contract, Legal aspect of the employment contract, Legal aspect of NewCo's service contract with external employees, Legal aspects of grievances within the NewCo company, Legal aspect of a NewCo patent, Legal aspect of the NewCo patent license, Legal aspect of NewCo IP-Assignments, Legal aspects of NewCo land ownership, Legal aspect of NewCo terminations, Legal aspects of social security of NewCo, Legal Aspect of NewCo strategy application contract, Legal aspect of a supplier contract of NewCo, Legal aspect of the tax application contract of NewCo, Legal aspect of the target strategy application contract, Legal aspect of the tax application contract, Legal aspect of the GTM Application Contract, Legal aspect of target MD contract, Legal risk of the target, Legal aspect of an IT service provider contract of the target, Legal aspects of target IT software contracts, Legal aspect of the target's hardware contract, Legal aspect of the target terminations, Legal aspect of the target's service contract with external employees, Legal aspects of complaints to the target company, Legal aspect of the patent license, Legal aspects of social insurance, Legal aspect regarding regulatory authorities, Legal aspect of IP assignment, Legal aspects of target land ownership, Legal aspects of the target rental agreement, Legal aspects of the employment contract, Legal aspect of target taxes, Legal aspect of the license contract to the partner, Legal aspect of a patent, Legal aspect of a brand or trademark, Legal aspect of an IP licensing contract, Legal aspect of an insurance contract, Legal aspect of a target customer contract, Legal aspect of a target partner contract, Legal aspect of a supplier contract, Legal aspect, Draft Legal Integration Plan, Laws

Automatability

This task is partially automatable.

9.7 Task Tax integration

Task description

During the process of merger integration, the aspect of tax integration assumes a pivotal role in facilitating a fluid transition while enhancing financial efficacy. This necessitates the harmonization of the tax strategies employed by the merging organizations to maximize tax advantages and mitigate liabilities. Such a procedure mandates a comprehensive evaluation of the pre-existing tax frameworks and compliance mechanisms to discern potential synergies and risks. Proficient tax integration can result in substantial cost reductions and augmented cash flow management for the newly constituted entity. Furthermore, it aids in ensuring adherence to tax regulations across various jurisdictions, consequently diminishing the likelihood of legal entanglements.

Attributes of the Task

The task is a decision task.

The task problem is structured.

The task has the following goal(s):

☐ Draft tax integration plan: executed

☐ Operations of target tax activities: aligned

☐ Target tax processes: aligned

The task has the following objectives:

☐ Tax synergy: maximized

☐ Tax costs of NewCo: minimized

☐ Tax risk of NewCo: minimized

The task consists of the following actions

☐ Conduct a thorough review of the tax implications of the merger

☐ Identify potential tax risks and opportunities

☐ Develop a detailed tax integration strategy

❏ Coordinate with tax advisors and legal counsel to ensure tax compliance

❏ Assess the impact of the transaction on various tax subjects like net operating losses and tax credits

❏ Determine the optimal tax structure for the combined entity

❏ Implement tax planning strategies to minimize tax cost and optimize cash flow

❏ Communicate the tax implications of the transaction to stakeholders

❏ Monitor and evaluate the effectiveness of the tax integration plan

❏ Continuously review and update the tax integration plan

The task works on the following data object types, among others:

Tax aspects of NewCo, Legal aspect of NewCo taxes, Tax aspect of NewCo customer contracts, Tax aspect of NewCo employment contracts, Tax aspect of NewCo's external employees, Tax aspect of the NewCo hardware contract, Tax aspect of NewCo's insurance contracts, Tax aspect of NewCo's IP licensing, Tax Aspects of NewCo's Application Contract, Tax aspect of NewCo's IT service provider contract, Tax aspects of NewCo leases, Tax aspect of the NewCo MD Contract, Tax aspect of NewCo partner contracts, Tax aspect of NewCo's outlicensing contracts, Tax aspect of a NewCo NewCo patent license, Tax aspect of NewCo patents, Tax aspect of the NewCo non-cash benefits, Tax aspect of NewCo IP-Assignment, Fiscal aspects of NewCo real estate, Tax aspect of NewCo's termination agreement, Tax aspect of NewCo social security, Tax aspect of NewCo supplier contracts, Contracts for NewCo tax applications, Legal aspect of the tax application contract of NewCo, Costs for NewCo Tax Applications, NewCo's tax applications, Tax audits of NewCo, Correspondence of NewCo with tax authorities, Tax costs of NewCo, Tax disputes of NewCo, Tax returns of NewCo, Tax litigation of NewCo, Tax matters of NewCo, Operations of NewCo's tax activities, Scheduled NewCo tax payments, Tax planning of NewCo, NewCo tax processes, Tax Refunds of NewCo, Tax risk of NewCo,

Tax aspects of NewCo transfer prices, Tax aspect of NewCo sales tax, Legal aspect of the tax application contract, Dispute regarding taxes, Tax litigation of the target, Tax planning of the target, Planned target tax payments, Tax authority, Tax returns of the target, Tax refunds, Tax audits of the target, Correspondence of the target with tax authorities, Tax aspect of a target patent license, Tax aspect of target social security, Tax aspect of the target IP assignment, Tax aspect of the target real estate, Tax aspect of the target leasing contracts, Tax aspect of target employment contracts, Tax aspect of target outbound license agreements, Tax aspect of the target patents, Tax aspect of the IP licensing of the target, Tax aspect of the target's insurance contracts, Tax aspect of the target customer contracts, Tax aspect of the target partner contracts, Tax aspect of target supplier contracts, Tax aspects of the target, Results of the target tax Due Diligence, Legal aspect of target taxes, Draft tax integration plan, Buyer taxes, Tax aspects, Target company tax

Automatability

This task is partially automatable.

9.8   Task IP integration

Task description

The post-merger integration of intellectual property (IP) comprises a methodical approach to harmonizing, consolidating, and administering the intellectual property assets belonging to two merging entities. This undertaking is paramount for optimizing the value of the unified organization s IP portfolio while ensuring adherence to pertinent statutes and regulations, including those that govern patents, trademarks, and copyrights. Essential activities within this framework encompass the identification and assessment of IP assets to ascertain their strategic significance and potential vulnerabilities, such as redundant patents or conflicting trademarks. Moreover, the integration process necessitates the negotiation and allocation of IP rights, guaranteeing that ownership and usage entitlements are distinctly articulated and congruent with the newly established corporate framework. The safeguarding of proprietary technologies and trade secrets also emerges as a central concern, necessitating efforts to align confidentiality agreements and security measures. The efficacious post-merger integration of IP plays a vital role in preserving competitive advantage, stimulating innovation, and mitigating the likelihood of IP-related conflicts within the integrated organization.

Attributes of the Task

The task is a decision task.

The task problem is structured.

The task has the following goal(s):

☐ Draft IP Integration Plan: executed

The task has the following objectives:

☐ Target's risks regarding intellectual property: minimized

☐ NewCo's risks regarding intellectual property: minimized

The task consists of the following actions

☐ Identify potential conflicts between the IP assets of the merging companies. is automated by 1 tool(s).

☐ Source, prepare, and collect all necessary IP documentation. is automated by 1 tool(s).

☐ Conduct a thorough valuation and due diligence of the IP assets. is automated by 1 tool(s).

☐ Develop IP integration plans and strategies. is automated by 1 tool(s).

☐ Ensure compliance with all IP-legal requirements and regulations. is not automated.

☐ Align the IP portfolios of the merging entities. is automated by 1 tool(s).

☐ Verify the chain of title and ownership of all IP assets. is automated by 1 tool(s).

☐ Establish processes for the ongoing management and protection of the assets. is not automated.

The task works on the following data object types, among others:

IP Licensing Contract, Legal aspect of a NewCo IP licensing contract, Tax aspect of NewCo's IP licensing, NewCo Partner Agreements, IP Assignments of NewCo, Legal aspect of NewCo IP-Assignments, Tax aspect of NewCo IP-Assignment, Tax aspect of the target IP assignment, Tax aspect of the IP licensing of the target, Partner agreements of the target, Legal aspect of IP assignment, IP-Assignments of the target, Legal aspect of an IP licensing contract, IP licensor, IP licensing contracts, NewCo's risks regarding intellectual property, Target's risks regarding intellectual property, Draft IP Integration Plan

Automatability

This task is partially automatable.

10. ABRAMS world trade wiki and PMI

Dr. Jürgen Abrams

inigma LLC. ABRAMS world trade wiki is a division of inigma LLC

Post-merger integration (PMI) is key to realizing synergies from M&A. This section explains the primary goals and challenges of integration.

10.1 Why ABRAMS world trade wiki for PMI?

With the invaluable assistance and comprehensive resources provided by the ABRAMS world trade wiki, one can delve deeply into a multitude of strategies aimed at effectively integrating the intricate networks of suppliers and customers that underpin the global marketplace.

The insights gleaned from this powerful tool enable a thorough discussion surrounding not only the potential cost synergies that may arise from such integrations but also the opportunities for revenue growth that could significantly enhance overall profitability, as well as the various methods for optimizing distribution channels to ensure efficiency and effectiveness in reaching end consumers.

ABRAMS world trade wiki offers a wealth of market insights specifically designed to facilitate a greater degree of strategic alignment among stakeholders while simultaneously fostering processes that lead to meaningful value creation in a highly competitive environment.

10.2 Strategic Goals of Integration with ABRAMS world trade wiki

This section discusses the strategic objectives of PMI, such as cost synergies, revenue growth, and fostering innovation. A critical aspect of achieving these objectives is identifying potential synergies arising from the combined market positions of the two merged companies. The following steps and criteria can help in this analysis:

Analyze Supplier Networks

Evaluating the supplier base is essential to uncover opportunities for synergy:

☐ **Distribution Channel Optimization**: Merged entities can streamline and integrate their distribution networks, removing inefficiencies such as overlapping routes or redundant logistical hubs, leading to cost savings and faster delivery times.

☐ **Overlaps in Distribution Networks**: By identifying and addressing overlaps, companies can consolidate distribution points, resulting in reduced operational costs and better resource utilization.

☐ **Exploiting Purchasing Power**: Combining procurement activities allows the merged entity to leverage increased purchasing volume, which can lead to improved negotiation power with suppliers, bulk discounts, and better payment terms.

Analyze Customer Networks

Understanding and integrating customer networks offers significant growth and retention potential:

☐ **Overlaps in Customer Bases**: Analyzing customer overlaps enables the merged company to streamline account management, avoid duplication of efforts, and focus on delivering tailored services to retain loyalty.

☐ **Sales Power Enhancement**: The combined market presence of the merged entity provides opportunities to cross-sell products or services across the expanded customer base, increasing revenue and deepening relationships.

☐ **Customer Retention Strategies**: A strong focus on retaining key customers by leveraging the strengths of both companies—such as improved service offerings or better pricing—helps to maintain and expand the customer base.

Market Position Analysis

Conducting a detailed review of the market positions of both companies highlights competitive advantages and areas for growth:

❑ **Identify Competitive Advantages**: The merger may create unique opportunities to combine strengths, such as complementary product portfolios or enhanced innovation capabilities, establishing a stronger market presence.

❑ **Address Market Gaps**: By analyzing the market position, companies can identify gaps in their offerings or geographic coverage and use the merger to fill these voids, creating a more robust and comprehensive market presence.

❑ **Enhance Brand Positioning**: Integrating branding strategies ensures a unified and stronger brand image, capitalizing on the reputation and strengths of both entities to solidify market leadership.

Here is an example regarding Company Transparency: The specifics concerning the shipment details that illustrate the principal customer countries associated with a hypothetical merger and acquisition target company, which specializes in exporting coating products, include notable countries such as Vietnam, India, and Indonesia, each of which plays a significant role in the company's overall market strategy and revenue generation.

16,356 entries found

Shipment	Supplier	Country	Customer	Country	Notify Party	Product Description	HS Code
1 2025-01-31 (registration)	Ppg Coatings Belgium bv	Unknown Country, Company Identified	Ppg Industries Inc. Area Economica Panama Pacifici 9097, Unidad B			PINTURA	320890190090
2 2025-01-28 (registration)	Ppg Coatings Belgium bv	Unknown Country, Company Identified	Ppg Industries Inc. Area Economica Panama Pacifici 9097, Unidad B			PINTURA	320890190090
3 2025-01-22 (arrival)	Ppg Wonwag Coatings GmbH & Co. KG Strohgaustr. 28, Stuttgart	Germany	Wonwag Coatin 3420 Kossuth S Lafayette, IN 47			PAINTS AND COLOURS	321290
4 2025-01-22 (arrival)	Ppg Wonwag Coatings GmbH & Co. KG Strohgaustr. 28, Stuttgart	Germany	Wonwag Coatin 3420 Kossuth S Lafayette, IN 47			DANGEROUS GOODSUN 1263 CL 3, IIUN 1866 CL 3, III	282710 e
5 2025-01-22 (arrival)	Ppg Woenwag Coatings GmbH & Co. KG Thomas-Dachser-Str. 1, Dachser Warehouse Malsch	Germany	Wonwag Coatin 3420 Kossuth S Lafayette, IN 47			DANGEROUS GOODSUN 1263 CL 3, IIUN 1866 CL 3, III	321290
6 2025-01-08 (arrival)	Ppg Coatings Belgium Bv/ S.R.L. Brusselchaussee De Haecht 1465 1130 Haren	Belgium	Ppg Industries I And 11505 Highway 77571 LA Porte			845 DRUMS ON 36 PALLETS BEING PAINT AND PAINT RELATED MATERIAL 75 DRUM S GUARD CSF 585 HRD 000000EUM50 UN 3 066, PAINT, 8, III, EMS F A, S B 154 DRUM S PRIME 200 K BAS YEL/GREEN 400900E UN 1263, PAINT, 3, III, (30 C C.C.), EMS F E, S E 88 DRUM S PRIME 200 K BAS GREY 951505E UN 126 …	32082090, 32089091, 390939
7 2025-01-08 (arrival)	Ppg Coatings Belgium Bv/ S.R.L. Brusselchaussee De Haecht 1465 1130 Haren	Belgium	Ppg Industries I And 11505 Highway 225 77571 LA Porte TX	America		1157 DRUMS ON 36 PALLETS BEING 72 DRUM S MU LT/PASTE SUPER RED YELL 3610MPEU1500 UN 1263, PAINT, 3, III, (31 C C.C), EMS P E, S E 44 DRUM S DUR ONE GREEN N419905EU2200 UN 1263, PAINT, 3, III, (31 C C.C), EMS F E, S E 12 0 DRUM S COLORANT ALX WHITE 706 070601EU1250 U…	32081090, 32082090, 32082010, 32089091, 321290, 140490

Customer Country ✕

	Shipments
Africa (8)	474 ⌃
🏴 Namibia	253
🇳🇬 Nigeria	73
🏴 Botswana	69
🏴 Cote D'Ivoire	63
🏴 Lesotho	8
🏴 Ghana	4
🏴 Angola	3
🏴 Liberia	1
Asia (22)	7,984 ⌃
🇻🇳 Viet Nam	2,615
🇮🇳 India	1,790
🇮🇩 Indonesia	950
🇵🇭 Philippines	769
🇸🇬 Singapore	398
🇰🇷 South Korea	263

GO

Figure 36: Company Transparency: Shipment details showing the main customer countries of a theoretical M&A target company

Scan this QR code to view the figure online.

Next, we present additional details about the notion of Company Transparency, particularly focusing on the specifics of shipment data that highlight the main countries that are significant buyers for a hypothetical target company engaged in mergers and acquisitions (M&A) within the coating products export sector, where the primary customer nations identified are the Russian Federation and India.

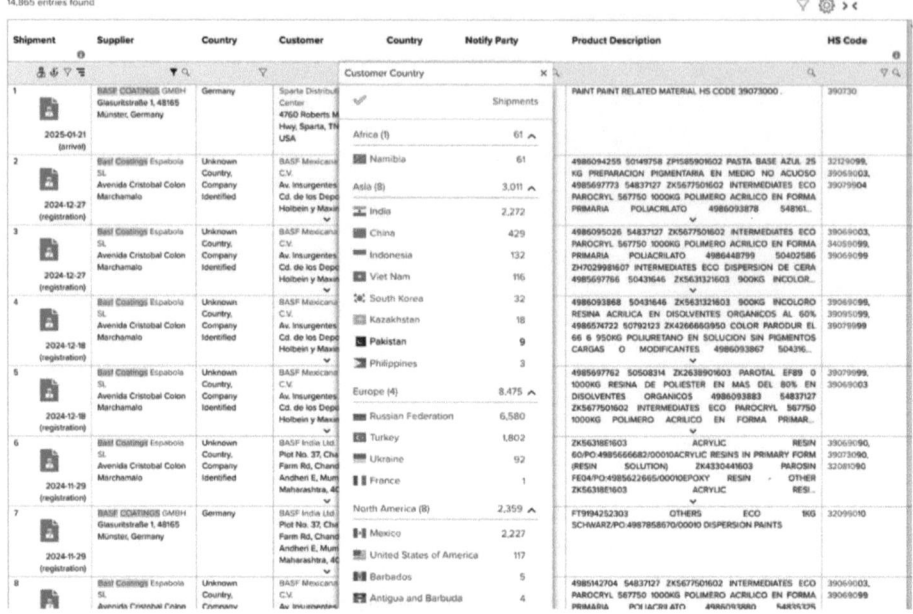

Figure 37: Company Transparency: Shipment details showing the main customer countries of another theoretical M&A target company

 Scan this QR code to view the figure online.

This detailed analysis not only aids in defining the strategic goals of integration but also ensures that the merger delivers maximum value through well-identified and actionable synergies. A critical aspect of achieving these objectives is identifying potential synergies arising from the combined market positions of the two merged companies.

11. PATEV for Post Merger Integration

Dr.-Ing. Edelbert Häfele, Dr.-Ing. Klaus Illgner-Fehns, Dr.-Ing. Judit Inacsovszky

PATEV Associates GmbH

The integration of intellectual property (IP) in business mergers extends beyond simply combining patent portfolios—it can lead to significant strategic advantages and new market opportunities.

11.1 IP – Business Integration: Synergies and how they lead to New Market Applications

Figure 38: EY Strategy&Transaction GmbH, Dr. Georg Beckmann: B&I Journey, part 3

Even when the transaction is done and integration follows as the last step in the M&A process, some aspects with respect to IP should be considered. The result is more than just the combination of two patent portfolios.

One aspect is the necessity to review the entire combined portfolio in detail. It might happen that the position in some technological areas gains substantially in relevance leading to a much stronger market position. Note that there are no identical patents. Patents may address the same technological area and share certain elements, but they always differ in coverage. Therefore, it is important to create an understanding of how the coverage of a technological area increases by the combination of the two patent portfolios. The effect gets apparent in the heatmap created by PATEV's Innovation Intelligence.

11.2 Leveraging heatmaps in IP Integration

Heatmaps are used to compare the number of patents of companies in certain technological areas. The heatmap in the next figure shows that the portfolio of Siemens and VARIAN are almost complementary in the technological area A and c3. The numbers denote the number of patents in each technological category. The combination creates substantial value. It not only increases the protection of products but creates also new opportunities for licensing.

Applicants - Analysis of hot and white spots

Applicant	A	a1	a1.1	a2	a3	a3.1	B	b1	b2	b3	C	c1	c2	c3	c3.1	Total
Koninklijke Philips NV	19	16	14	1	4	4	29	7			24	42	20	12	10	87
Siemens AG	6	1	1	2	3	1	40	21	3	20	41	25	11	5		83
Elekta Ab	27	21	19	5	9	9	3	1		2	21	6	3	14	1	43
Varian Medical Systems, Inc.	21	18	10	4	10	4	2	1		1	24	1	6	18	4	39
Hitachi, Ltd.	15	12	7	1	5	3					13	1	1	12	1	25
Brainlab AG	15	6	5	4	12	4	7	2		5	2		1	1		18
Samsung Electronics Co., Ltd.							8	1		7	12	10	2			18
Ion Beam Applications Sa	9	4	1		6	2	1			1	12	2	2	8		17
Toshiba Corporation	11	8	5	5	2	1	4	2			3	4		4		14
Accuray Incorporated	10	8	7	1	4	4	2	2	2	2	9	1	4	5		11
General Electric Company							3	1			2	6	3	3		9
Mevion Medical Systems, Inc.	4	3	2	2	2						7			7		9
Medtronic Plc	1		1				3	2	1		4	1	3			8
Neuboron Medtech Ltd.	5	5	3								4			4	1	8
Total	220	150	111	36	86	49	167	59	32	92	447	187	130	142	19	748

Figure 39: Heatmap based on the number of patent families of companies in three technological areas A, B, C, including a selected number of technical categories. Screenshot PATEV Innovation Intelligence Showcase Report VARIAN.

This extension of coverage may not only apply to the key technological areas investigated during due diligence, but specifically for larger portfolios, this could apply also to other technological areas. A broader coverage of technological areas may also allow to license a broader scope to manufacturing partners or even other market participants.

It is worthwhile to cross-check if protected technologies in the new portfolio could apply to different applications and use cases. Analyze the portfolio in the light of the new strategic direction of the company and market scope. „Innovation Intelligence" can be used to support this analysis.

11.3 Determine merger impact on key innovation fields

Another aspect is to check if the key innovation fields overall have changed by this merger. It might happen that for some non-core technological areas the position of the merged company gets much stronger. A larger portfolio with a higher relevance pushes the company in the diagram to the right making it a stronger market participant. The position for negotiations, for instance for cross-licensing, gets much better. It may turn out that this technological area is not in the scope of the company anymore. But a stronger and more relevant portfolio allows us to negotiate better licensing or selling conditions. Consequently, for all technological areas covered by the new merged portfolio an "innovation intelligence" should check its new relevance and coverage.

Inventions and innovation flourish only if the culture and environment of a company recognizes and appreciates innovation. Inventions and innovation must be appreciated by the management. The management must clearly communicate that innovations and patents are a key element in its strategic positioning. And it must become apparent to the employes that patents contribute to the value and commercial success of the company. A key task will be to make sure that this spirit prevails in the newly merged organization.

Something one might easily oversee is that inventive ideas require highly skilled employees with the drive to invent. Roughly speaking there are two types of inventors. Some call for an environment with little constraints where they can basically work freely on topics, more like university researchers. Here, disruptive new ideas are likely to be invented. Companies need to sell products and services for which permanent innovations are needed. This requires that innovators understand market demand and market developments and are integrated into the strategic positioning of the company.

Whatever the type of inventor, it is vital for the new company to identify and retain key inventors. Their knowledge and expertise are needed to exploit the technology claimed in the patents. It is therefore particularly important to keep the inventors of the acquired company on board. They should feel comfortable and be assured that the innovation-friendly environment they know will remain intact. Experienced innovators are multipliers in the company and help to train other colleagues. It is important to monitor the integration of two companies from this point of view as well.

Although companies should have the means to identify key innovators from their HR databases, this may not be trivial, especially in large companies. Patent research is an efficient way to easily identify the key innovators. The next figure analyses the inventors of the patents filed by VARIAN. It appears that there are at least 20 key people who have contributed to at least 15 patents. Note that patents usually have several inventors. Cross-checking the names with internal employment records would then allow their current role and position to be identified and provide incentives for them to stay in the company.

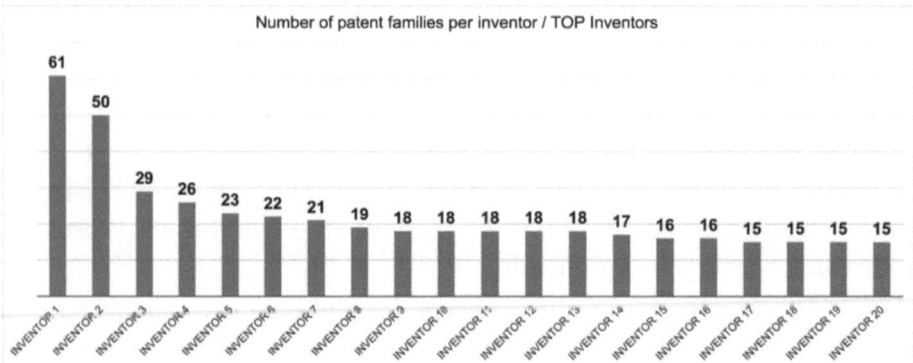

Figure 40: Number of inventions per inventor, PATEV Innovation Intelligence Showcase Report VARIAN

In conclusion, a detailed review of the merged portfolio is essential to understand the enhanced technological coverage and its impact on market positioning. Tools like heatmaps can reveal complementary strengths.

Moreover, the merger may shift the company's position in key innovation fields, potentially strengthening its bargaining power for cross-licensing and negotiations. Beyond the technical aspects, fostering an innovation-driven culture is critical for sustaining long-term success. Retaining key inventors from the acquired company ensures continuity in innovation, as their expertise is vital for leveraging the newly integrated IP. Identifying these innovators through patent research and incentification their retention can maximize the value derived from the merger.

12. The companies behind Disruptive automation of M&A

Dr. Karl Michael Popp

Corpvision.ai combines the strength of four companies to create disruptive automation for the M&A process. This section provides details about Corpvision.ai, its companies and a combined M&A scenario.

12.1 Corpvision.ai

The days of massive manual work in corporate development to evaluate business opportunities are over. Corpvision.AI provides full automation to bring together four dimensions of corporate development work. Each of the dimensions is covered with a market leading tool as well as with specific, one-of-a-kind content for each of the four dimensions:

❐ Supply chain intelligence (provided by ABRAMS world trade wiki),

❐ IP and Patent intelligence (provided by PATEV),

❐ B2B Market intelligence and simulation (provided by Modelyzr),

❐ Business ecosystem intelligence (provided by Coveritas).

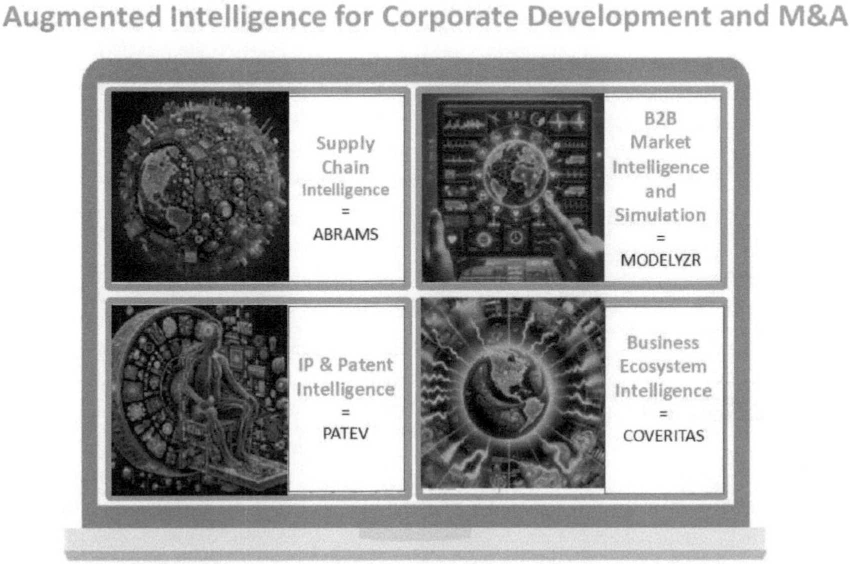

Augmented Intelligence for Corporate Development and M&A

Figure 41: Corpvision.ai dimensions and tools define augmented intelligence

By combining the four dimensions, a holistic view of a company can be automatically generated and help corporate development professionals to not only work smarter and faster, but also with higher precision. We call this augmented intelligence. Now let us have a look at each of the dimensions and tools.

While ABRAMS and PATEV have already been introduced in this book, let us introduce Modelyzr and Coveritas.

12.2 Market intelligence and simulation with Modelyzr

Corporate development professionals often ask themselves questions regarding the addressed market, the size of the addressable market but also how much of the addressable market can be converted into revenue.

Generative AI Market Model to predict market impact

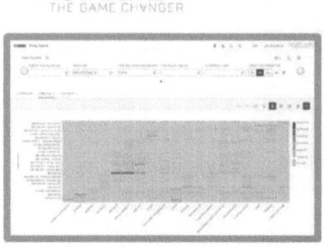

* **Generative B2B AI Market Model for way better Go-to-Market**
* Digitize Market Research, Market Analytics and Targeting
* Predict and Maximize Customer Lifetime Value
* Simulate and Analyze Markets, drill down into market segments
* Full market analysis, detailed estimation of Selling-Potential
* SAP Industry Cloud certified solution / Available in SAP Store
* Modelyzr is successfully used by global B2B services companies with 3.000+ Users in Marketing, Sales, Channel & Management and 100+ Countries worldwide

www.modelyzr.com

AI-Technologies:
* Generative Market Model
* Machine Learning and specialized AI algorithms
* Algorithms trained & optimized with billions of productive enterprise data sets
* Integrations with 60 data sources incl. e.g. SAP S4/Hana, ERP, CRM, CX, D&B, Outreach, Dealroom and many more
* 100% built & run on SAP BTP, Hana, S4/Hana etc.

Figure 42: Modelyzr

The activities connected to this are market modelling and simulation of markets or prognosis of company revenues in such market, which today are highly manual activities. Modelyzr changes the game by leveraging many data sources and an AI-driven simulation of market impact by customer, by industry, by country or overall.

12.3 Business ecosystem intelligence with Coveritas

What is the business ecosystem of a company, which customers, suppliers, partners, competitors make up this ecosystem? What are recent events and news within this ecosystem and how do you make sense of it? Sounds like a lot of manual work, but it isn´t anymore.

These are questions where Coveritas with its unique automatic data collection comes to help. As soon as you have defined a company or an industry or any topic of your interest, a swarm of data-collecting agents automatically collects and correlates information about the company, industry or topic in real time. Watch the ecosystem of companies and relationships build up before you and run further analysis on the topic like sentiment analysis.

Business Ecosystem Insights in Realtime

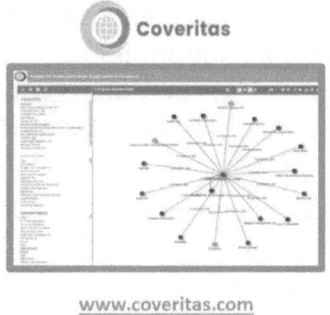

Coveritas

- Automatically Discover Business Ecosystems in "real-time"
- Gain Insights into the "unknown" of potential target companies
- Monitor actual events via news analysis
- Complementary add-on technology to ABRAMS, MODELYZR and PATEV
- Built on a highly scalable micro-agent-platform - let hundred-thousands of micro-agents (similar to ants) do the job for you, leveraging NLP and micro-knowledge-graphs and further AI-technologies.

www.coveritas.com

Developed by team from:

AI-Technologies:
- Micro-Agent/Robot-Platform with 100.000s of microagents
- agent-to-agent communication via micro-knowledge graphs
- Natural Language Processing incl. sentiment analytics
- usage of e.g. ChatGPT to reduce and simplify human actions

Figure 43: Coveritas

12.4 Joint Demo Scenario of the four tools

Analyzing acquisition opportunities entails the analysis of data concerning companies, partners, competitors, markets, patents, and supply chains of potential entities. Typically, this process is characterized by being laborious and requiring manual input. However, by utilizing CORPVISION AI, you can streamline and automate this process.

Hence, we demonstrate how CORPVISION AI, our innovative technology suite designed for M&A and corporate development initiatives, integrates data on companies, partners, competitors, markets, patents, and supply chains with cutting-edge technologies to assess and evaluate acquisitions during the M&A strategy and due diligence phases.

In this demonstration scenario, we assist an automotive manufacturer in enhancing their assisted and autonomous driving solutions through the assessment of potentially acquiring a 4D-Radar technology firm.

Step 1: Analyzing the space

In the initial step of the process, the examination of analytics related to patents and intellectual property serves as a valuable initial step that furnishes you with a solid foundational framework, revealing various industry incumbents actively engaged in the development of specific technologies and patent portfolios.

Our proprietary PATEV technology empowers you to conduct an automated evaluation and comparison of both current and prospective technological advancements. Our approach commences with a comprehensive evaluation of the technology space encompassing autonomous driving technologies. First, we select 4D radar technology as the corresponding patent family to research in.

PATEV

Methodology - Structuring

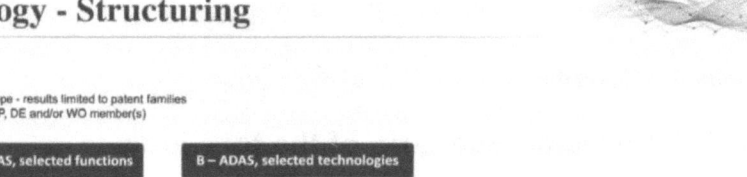

Figure 44: Corpvision.ai analyzing the space

Then we see the list of companies (applicants) that have applied for patents in this patent family.

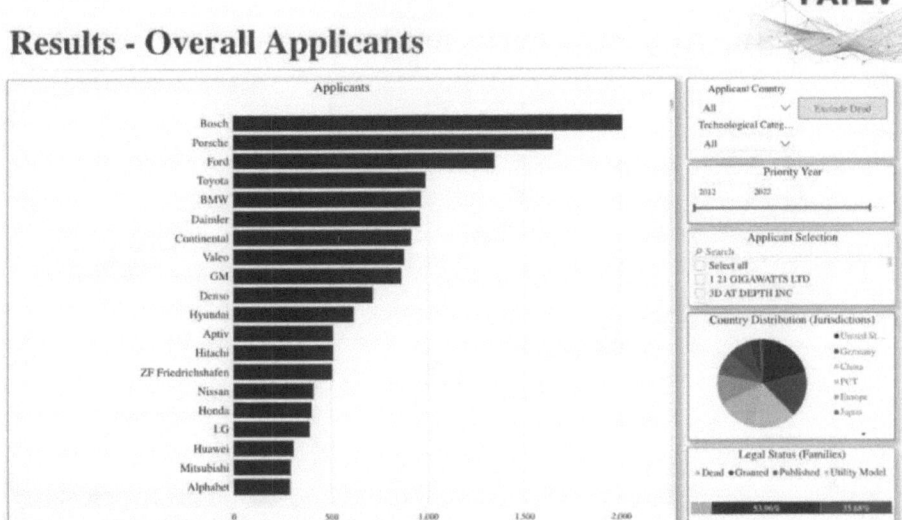

Figure 45: Corpvision.ai Applicants view

This preliminary assessment is followed by a more in-depth exploration into the domain of 4D-Radar technology, wherein we analyze and compare the various stakeholders operating in this space, ultimately identifying APTIV as a promising candidate for further consideration and exploration.

Results - Top Applicant Performance

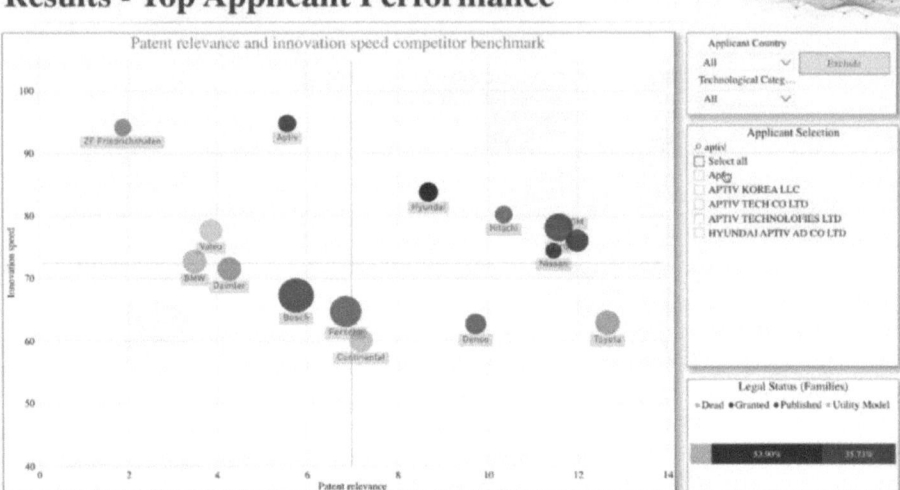

Figure 46: Corpvision.ai Applicant performance

Here, we can already see Aptiv in the upper middle section. Aptiv shows high innovation speed and good patent relevance. So, Aptiv might be a good target for acquisition. But how can we get more information about this company, e.g. about its competitors.

Step 2: Business ecosystem analysis

As a next step, it is our intention to explore and evaluate the yet unfamiliar business ecosystem of APTIV. This is achieved through an analysis of the business data and relationships pertaining to the company APTIV.

Our COVERITAS technology automatically recognizes potential partners, competitors, and comparable companies, initiating the formation of a business ecosystem.

Moreover, it commences the monitoring of the business ecosystem by utilizing internet and company data, facilitated by its highly adaptable micro-agent-network, operating nearly in real-time.

Here, we switch to Coveritas to immediately see the competitors of the company.

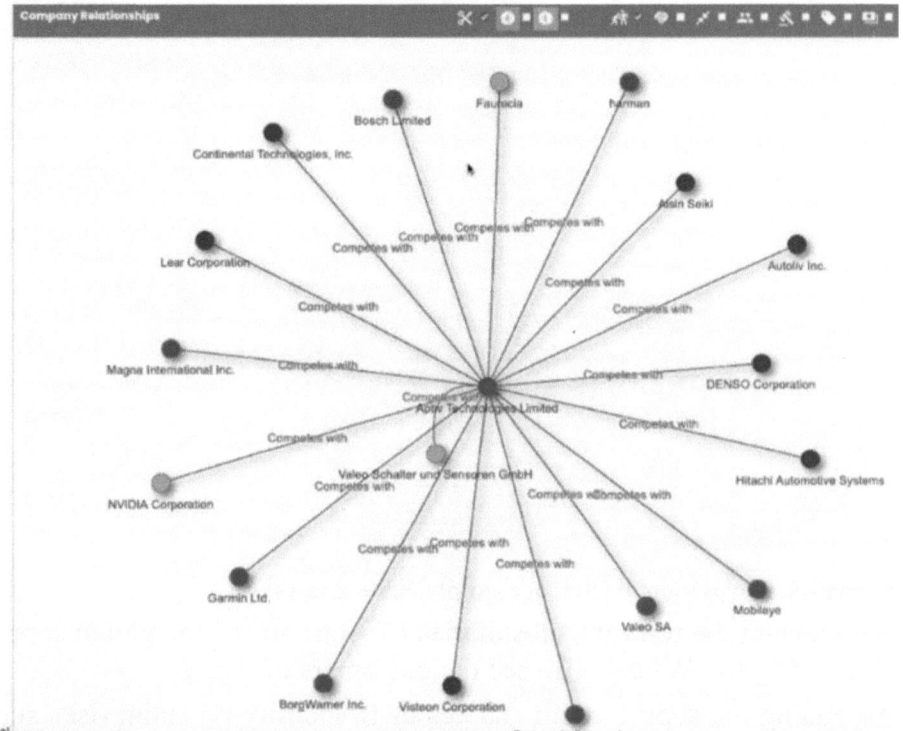

Figure 47: Corpvision.ai business ecosystem analysis

So, we know that Aptiv is innovative at a high speed and we know its competitors. But what about the supply chain of Aptiv? Here we switch to ABRAMS world trade wiki.

Step 3: Supply chain analysis

Let us now proceed to investigate the supply chain of APTIV.

Our ABRAMS technology provides us with a comprehensive understanding of the APTIV suppliers, clients, shipments, and the estimated monetary value of transactions between them.

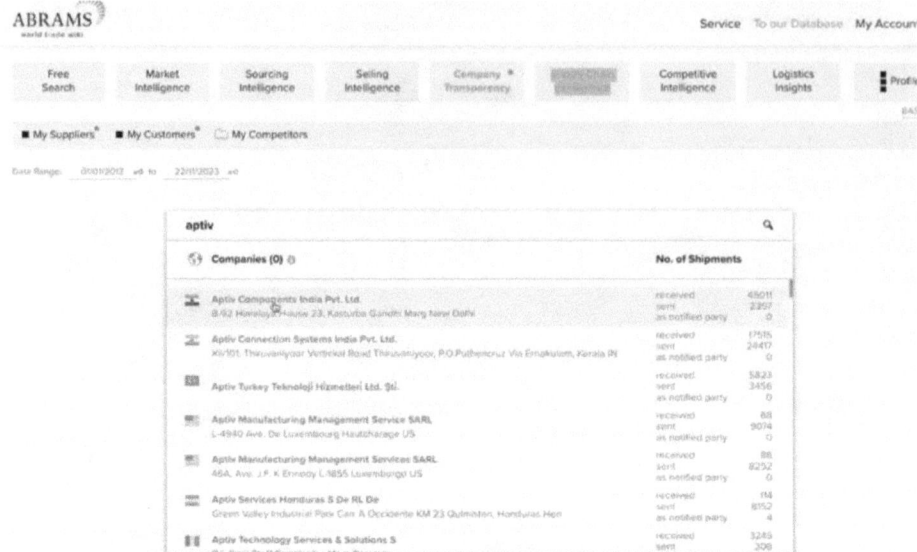

Figure 48: Corpvision.ai coverage supply chain analysis 1

We selected the relevant subsidiaries of Aptiv to see the global supply chain of Aptiv. We can also see the customers of Aptiv.

Ascending the supply chain enables us to identify potential risks such as embargoes or regulatory concerns like child labor within the APTIV supply chain, including suppliers of APTIV suppliers.

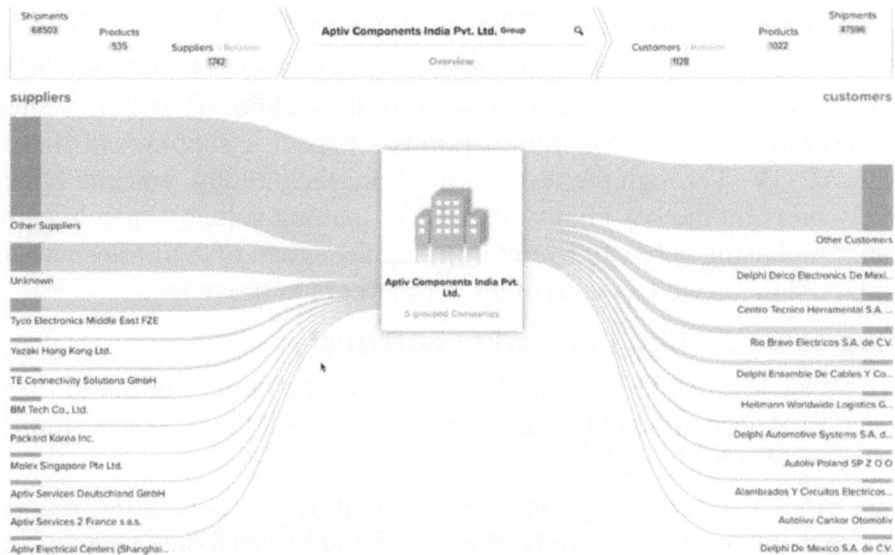

Figure 49: Corpvision.ai supply chain analysis 2

During our demonstration utilizing authentic ABRAMS data, we promptly observe that certain APTIV suppliers are situated in Taiwan, posing a risk due to the current geopolitical climate.

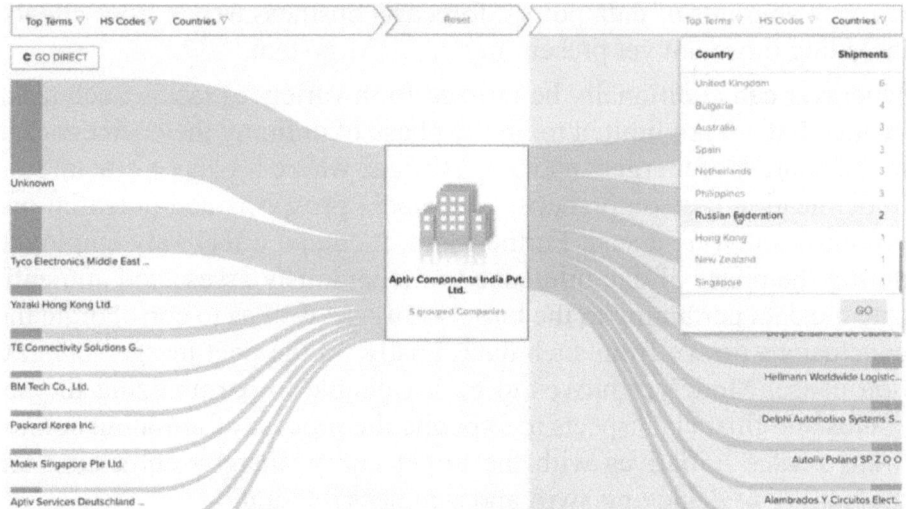

Figure 50: Corpvision.ai supply chain analysis 3

Furthermore, we note that APTIV maintains active clientele in Russia, presenting an even more significant concern in the occidental sphere.

Our advanced ABRAMS technology provides additional benefits, such as the ability to locate substitute options for specific suppliers affiliated with APTIV. Through the utilization of our technology, you can effectively pinpoint the key clients of APTIV, gaining valuable insights into their purchasing behavior by determining the extent of their transactions with APTIV as well as with other competitors in the industry.

Step 4: Evaluating the market potential

We go back to PATEV technology to study the larger market for 'Assisted or Autonomous Driving' and aim to assess the business significance of acquiring APTIV.

Our Modelyzr technology utilizes an AI-powered generative market model that harnesses a variety of internal and external data sources, including but not limited to ABRAMS, Coveritas, PATEV, CRM systems, Dealroom, Dun & Bradstreet, ERP systems, HubSpot, Outreach, and other potentially integrated sources.

A sophisticated machine learning solution, which has been trained using vast amounts of data points, forecasts business trends from clients, including those not yet present in our CRM system.

Modelyzr can additionally be utilized for a variety of tasks. Such tasks include but are not limited to: in the phase of defining the business case in the context of mergers and acquisitions, where it plays a crucial role in delineating the comprehensive business prospects and potential opportunities that lie ahead. Furthermore, it can be effectively employed during the phase of due diligence to meticulously assess and authenticate the data pertaining to the target entity, as well as to corroborate the conclusions drawn from such data. Lastly, in the post-merger-integration phase, Modelyzr proves to be invaluable in harmonizing the accounts and financial aspects to expedite the process of initiating collaborative sales initiatives with the target entity, thereby enhancing the probability of achieving swift and seamless integration.

13. Future vision of M&A automation

Dr. Karl Michael Popp

In this section we would like to present the future vision of M&A automation. Well, to be honest, it is a vision of the near future since we will only leverage the technologies that exist today. Unfortunately, many of these technologies are not used for M&A processes yet.

To better grasp the ideas behind the future vision and to create requirements for existing tool vendors, we will add mock-ups of the future vision to each chapter.

Let us assume the vision gets implemented in a solution called M&ABot. M&ABot uses a library of successful strategies and business models. It also leverages quantum computing. Enjoy.

13.1 Real-time M&A strategy

Consider the data used by our bot to be all data about the buyer and target company, its suppliers, its markets, products, customers and competitors. M&ABot´s data are provided in realtime, and the functionality of M&ABot automates most of the tasks of the M&A strategy phase. Hence, it can provide evaluation and creation of strategies in real-time. It will provide updates of the strategic position of a company in real time and propose appropriate strategic actions to take based on realtime data of the company, its suppliers, customers, partners, competitors.

Determine the status quo of the buyer and getting ready for strategy planning.

M&ABot works based on a dataplane and creates an initial status of your company. It assembles, aligns and connects data from different data sources like the company´s ERP system, market data, data about competitors etc. to create a unified view of where the company stands. It also integrates data about customers, e.g. customer sentiment, and, of course, about similar potential customers out there in the market.

Drafting the growth strategy

You set a growth goal, e.g. a certain increase in revenue, say 45 percent, over the next two years. M&ABot analyses potential areas of growth and proposes areas to act upon based on data about the company, the customers, economic outlook data and competitors.

Based on the analysis of the scalability of the company´s business model, operational model and channels, M&ABot knows the limits of organic growth and predicts the future growth.

And if the growth is planned to be higher than organic growth opportunities, M&ABot proposes an inorganic move.

Evaluating the inorganic growth strategy

Again, M&ABot leverages a large amount of data about companies, markets, competitors, supply chains, patents etc. as well as data about successful execution of strategic moves together with genetic algorithms and machine learning to select and detail out the strategy that is most likely to succeed.

In the next step this strategy is discussed with the managers empowered to take the decision. Say, the decision is taken to make an inorganic move and find a target company to buy.

Finding and selecting the right target

Determining target fit is a multidimensional task, which can cover dimensions like size, location, market position, supply chain and customers, product portfolio, people, patents etc.

M&ABot checks all dimensions of thousands of companies in adjacent and remote markets as well as up and down the supply chain. Besides other data, it leverages patent data to determine the strength of the patent portfolio and the innovation speed of targets. By doing this, a longlist is automatically created. Managers can then help M&ABot filter the list to create a shortlist.

Predicting the success of a potential acquisition

Let us assume that we have a simple definition of success: we would like to reach revenue targets for the acquisition. Then, M&ABot, with the help of Modelyzr, can predict the revenue that can be reached post-close with the acquired products. This information helps to decide which target to approach. Let us assume that one target is selected and willing to be acquired.

13.2 Real-time due diligence

The due diligence starts, and a data room has been populated with documents as requested by M&ABot. All contents of the data room are analyzed for completeness and consistency. They are subjected to an automatic and comprehensive analysis process that meticulously examines each element for a thorough understanding.

Real-time dashboards have it all

Moreover, there are dashboards that present a detailed listing of critical statistics, the overall completeness of the data, potential red flags that may indicate issues, as well as deal breakers that could jeopardize the transaction.

Knowledge graph has the red tape

M&ABot creates a knowledge graph over the data room information provided that tough questions like: "what is the holistic view on customer A, where the target currently has an escalation?" can be answered. Imagine the knowledge graph for customer A to be a red tape across all documents concerning the customer in the data room like revenue with the customer, contracts, support messages, pipeline etc. all this information is combined with each other to create a holistic view.

Do we still need questionnaires?

In addition, the questionnaires that were previously utilized for the due diligence process are now automatically answered by M&Abot based on the all-embracing content available in the data room plus additional data sources like market data, ensuring efficiency and accuracy in responses.

Furthermore, additional questions designed to probe deeper into any specific matters of concern are automatically generated and promptly communicated to both the target company and its advisors for further clarification and insight. Remember, on the target side there might be automated agents as well working on the information requests of the buyer.

Financial due diligence is automated

Financial due diligence is done automatically by M&Abot, based on standardized APIs to ERP and accounting systems, which allow access to financial data directly.

Frequent valuation possible

With the additional information that the buyer has now, the prediction of revenues can be rerun for a more precise evaluation of the synergies of the planned acquisition. Furthermore, the valuation of the target based on financial data, revenues, patent exploration and synergies from aligning supply chain and customer chain can be done as shown in this book. M&ABot automatizes this completely, so that the evaluation and valuation can be monitored frequently.

13.3 Merger integration

M&ABot is a set of software agents that interact with each other. Software agents based on agentic AI are massively assisting experts and take up most of the workload for merger integration. View software agents as subject matter experts and coworkers, not pieces of software. They assist in data collection and the processing of the data along the steps in the integration process.

Software agents can work on decision tasks, like deciding if the allowed number of vacation days are correct for each of the acquired employees before sending out new contracts to the acquired employees. They also keep track automatically of the progress of the integration project.

14. Results and Summary

Strategy formulation, validation and implementation have had a minimal degree of automation in the past decades. But numerous new tools and technologies provide a high degree of automation for many tasks and actions in this phase. This high degree of automation disrupts the way we are running M&A processes.

Due diligence activities increasingly get automated. Starting with "simple" automations like automatic blackening, feature extraction out of contracts the wave of innovation has just started. Today, whole financial due diligence activities can be widely automated already.

Complexity of merger integration activities can be daunting. Modern tools with AI can help by providing holistic information as red tapes through complexity. Starting now, software agents are taking over more and more of the integration work.

The authors and the editor of this book series are looking forward to further innovations and automation scenarios within book number two in this series, that will introduce two additional disruptive tools for automation of deals.

15. Literature

[FeSi,97] Modeling of business systems using the semantic object model (SOM) : a methodological framework. Bamberg: Otto-Friedrich-Univ., 1997.

 [Popp,20] Popp, K.M. Automation of Mergers and Acquisitions: Due Diligence Tasks and Automation (M&A Media Services Digitization M&A Vol. 1). BOD, Norderstedt, 2020

 [Popp,18] Popp, K.M. Mergers and Acquisitions in the Software Industry: Foundations of due diligence. BOD, Norderstedt, 2018.

[Popp,23] Popp, K.M. Automation of Mergers and Acquisitions: M&A Strategy Processes: Theory, Tasks and Automatability (M&A Media Services Digitization M&A Vol. 2). BOD, Norderstedt, 2023

[Popp,25] Popp, K.M. Automation of Mergers and Acquisitions: Merger integration: Theory, Tasks and Automatability (M&A Media Services Digitization M&A Vol. 3). BOD, Norderstedt, 2025, to be published

[Meyer,17] Meyer, R., Profit from the SAP Ecosystem: Business Models, Partnering, Go-to-Market. Books on Demand, Norderstedt, 2017.

[Smith,12] Smith, K., Lajoux, A.R., The Art of M&A Strategy. McGraw-Hill, New York, 2012.

16. Index

Karl Michael Popp (ed.): Automating the Deal Vol. 1

Karl Michael Popp (ed.): Automating the Deal Vol. 1

Karl Michael Popp (ed.): Automating the Deal Vol. 1